*Twayne's English Authors Series*

Sylvia E. Bowman, *Editor*
INDIANA UNIVERSITY

*Mark Rutherford*
*(William Hale White)*

(TEAS) 53

# Mark Rutherford
# (William Hale White)

By Stephen Merton
*The City College of New York*

Twayne Publishers, Inc.  ::  New York

*Copyright © 1967 by Twayne Publishers, Inc.*
All Rights Reserved

Library of Congress Catalog Card Number: 67-19342

MANUFACTURED IN THE UNITED STATES OF AMERICA

*To the memory of*
IRWIN EDMAN

# *Preface*

"Mark Rutherford" is a name that has continued to evoke a stream of tribute, sparse in volume but undiminished in impact, for over half a century. In 1886, shortly after William Hale White's second novel appeared, William Dean Howells extolled his work. Of Hale White's first two novels, Howells said that they "may yet mark a new era in fiction . . . they are so simply and nobly serious. . . . We could not give too strong an impression of their incomparable sincerity."[1] Writing of Hale White in 1910, Edmund Gosse observed: "It appears to us that no other author of anything like his rank has in our time been so continuously neglected by responsible criticism."[2] This statement is almost as true today as it was when Gosse wrote it, but with the recent growing interest in the Victorian period, Hale White's name has become somewhat better known. He died in 1913, at the end of an era, having lived for eighty-one years and having expressed the significant themes of his time with fullness, sureness, and restraint. During the last decade or more, scholarly studies about him have begun to appear. A biography and at least two doctoral dissertations, one on his fiction and the other on his religion and art, were published in the 1950's.

Though Hale White has never been popular or widely known, he has won the praise of such authors as D. H. Lawrence, Arnold Bennett, Joseph Conrad, Stephen Crane, and André Gide.[3] The praise has been of the sort one reserves for a new discovery. He is the kind of writer who appeals especially to a certain type of reader—to one who has lived an introspective life. Hale White's own intense need for privacy is evident in his passion for anonymity. He used, for example, one pseudonym to protect another: "Reuben Shapcott," the make-believe editor, presents to the world "Mark Rutherford." He denied his authorship of the novels with sharp finality. The reasons for his withdrawal are interesting, and they are woven into the very fabric of his work. This is a dominant motif I shall pursue in discussing his fiction.

In this study I show two sides of Hale White: the writer of distinctive novels and the representative Victorian. His novels present an aspect of Victorian culture that no other novelist has, by common consent, treated so adequately as he: the nonconformist, lower-middle-class life of small farmers, shopkeepers, printers, booksellers—the Puritan element in the Victorian milieu. Hale White conveys both the ardor, religious and political, of this class and the loss of its religious vitality under the impact of Victorian commercialism and prosperity. In doing so, Hale White becomes the only clear spokesman for this significant segment of Victorian society. His novels convey with intensity the modern sense of alienation—an intensity finely tempered by irony and rendered in transparent prose.

As the representative Victorian, Hale White is unusual in the variety of his work, which reflects diverse aspects of the intellectual and moral climate of the age. He was, for example, the standard translator of Spinoza's *Ethic*. He was a student of astronomy; scientific observations and papers are scattered throughout his journals. He was also a journalist, stationed in the House of Commons, who wrote weekly reports on the proceedings there for several decades of his life. In the course of these reports he touched on quite a number of the political and social topics of the time. This interest in political problems is intimately related to his religion—to the nonconformist outlook that combines religion with politics and that dates back to the days of Oliver Cromwell. All these activities of his I treat in this study. Wherever possible, I have pointed out analogies between Hale White's ideas and those of other authors of the nineteenth century.

Religion, politics, philosophy, science, and fiction, moreover, all cross-fertilize one another in his writings. I have consistently tried to show how, for example, his seminal concept of religion enters all his concerns, and how his fiction both reflects and illuminates his manifold interests.

Whenever feasible, I have relied on quotations from Hale White's writings rather than on a summary because these writings are not generally familiar or easily available. Moreover, only from such quotations can the flavor of the man and the period be adequately conveyed. ("I always look for the inverted commas," he himself says in regard to lecturers and essayists.)

*Preface*

Nonetheless, I have restricted my quotations to keep within the limits set for this book.

For the same reason I make no attempt to consider Hale White's intellectual interests in any detail. I omit practically all his criticism and scholarship, of which there is much, about individual authors. I touch only cursorily on his philosophy and political writing in Chapter 9.

STEPHEN MERTON

*The City College of New York*

# *Acknowledgments*

The material included in the first three chapters appeared originally, in different form, in the following articles: "The Autobiographical Novels of Mark Rutherford," *Nineteenth-Century Fiction*, V (December, 1950), 189-207; "The Personality of Mark Rutherford," *Nineteenth-Century Fiction*, VI (June, 1951), 1-20; "Mark Rutherford: The World of the Novels," *Bulletin of The New York Public Library*, LXVII (September, 1963), 470-78; "George Eliot and William Hale White," *The Victorian Newsletter*, No. 25 (Spring, 1964), 13-15. My thanks are due to the editors of these journals for permission to use material from these articles. (The articles in *Nineteenth-Century Fiction* © 1950 and 1951 by The Regents of the State of California, are reprinted in part with permission of The Regents.)

For grants that have aided me at various stages in the preparation of this work I thank The Committee on Research of The American Philosophical Society, The General Faculty Committee on Research of The City College of New York, and The Research Foundation of The City University of New York.

In the course of my work I have incurred personal obligations which it is a pleasure for me here to acknowledge. I wish to express my grateful thanks to Professors Morton Cohen and Arthur Zeiger of The City College of New York, who read my manuscript with careful critical attention. For encouragement and sponsorship of grant applications I owe a debt of gratitude to Professor Emeritus Mark Van Doren of Columbia University, to Professor Bradford A. Booth of the University of California at Los Angeles, to Professors Edgar Johnson, Samuel Middlebrook, Coleman Parsons, Harry Rudman, Oscar Sherwin, Edmond Volpe and Dean Oscar Zeichner, all of The City College of New York. Professors Sylvia Bowman and George Levine of Indiana University also have given me encouragement for which I am deeply grateful. To Professor Bowman for her meticulous editing I owe a further debt of gratitude. Finally, I want to thank Mr. Ronald Broudy, Mr. Fred Byron, Miss Marion Covell, Miss Alma Kadragic, and Mr. Stephen Melamed for typing and clerical assistance.

## Contents

Preface

Acknowledgments

Chronology 15

1. The Man and the Novels 21
2. Early Life: *The Autobiography of Mark Rutherford* 42
3. Later Life: *Mark Rutherford's Deliverance* 62
4. Politics and Religion: *The Revolution in Tanner's Lane* 75
5. Science and Religion: *Miriam's Schooling* 89
6. Love and Religion: *Catharine Furze* 103
7. Philosophy, Love and Religion: *Clara Hopgood* 120
8. Themes of the Fiction: The Short Stories 135
9. A Victorian Quest 140
10. Achievements 161

Notes and References 165

Selected Bibliography 181

Index 187

# *Chronology*

1831 William Hale White born on December 22 in Bedford, the son of William White, printer and bookseller.
1849 Met the Reverend Caleb Morris, the Independent minister who was greatly to influence him.
1850 Wrote to Carlyle and received a sympathetic letter in reply.
1851 Experienced a spiritual awakening upon reading Wordsworth in the *Lyrical Ballads*. In October he was transferred to the just opened New College, London, to continue his theological studies.
1852 Expelled from New College. In London he secured work with John Chapman, publisher of the *Westminster Review*.
1854 Obtained a post as clerk in the Registrar-General's Office in Somerset House.
1856 Married Harriet Arthur. Preached in Unitarian pulpits.
1858 Obtained a post as "Third Class Clerk" in the Accountant-General's Department in the Admiralty, where he was to stay until his retirement in 1892.
1860 First visit to Germany.
1861 Began his weekly articles, reporting for various provincial newspapers the debates in the House of Commons, an extra chore he continued until 1883.
1866 *An Argument for the Extension of the Franchise*, in support of the Liberal Reform Bill.
1868 Visited Carlyle.
1877 *A Letter Written on the Death of Mrs. Elizabeth Street* privately printed and circulated. "House Building," letter in the *Spectator*, reprinted in Ruskin's *Fors Clavigera*.
1879 Appointed Assistant Director of Contracts in the Admiralty. "Notes on Shelley's Birthplace," in *Macmillan's Magazine*.

1880 "The Genius of Walt Whitman," "Marcus Antoninus," "Ixion," and "Heathen Ethics," all published in *The Secular Review*.

1881 *The Autobiography of Mark Rutherford* published, as were all his novels, under the pseudonym of "Mark Rutherford." "The Mysterious Portrait," a short story, in *The Birmingham Post*. "Byron, Goethe, and Mr. Matthew Arnold" in *The Contemporary Review*. Visited Browning.

1883 Translation from the Latin of Spinoza's *Ethic*, completed more than twenty years before, published. Second visit to Germany.

1884 *A Dream of Two Dimensions*, a short story, printed for private circulation.

1885 *Mark Rutherford's Deliverance*, along with two essays, "Notes on the Book of Job" and "Principles."

1887 *The Revolution in Tanner's Lane*.

1889 Bought a telescope and started the study of astronomy.

1890 *Miriam's Schooling*.

1891 His wife died.

1892 Retired from the Admiralty on a £500 yearly pension.

1893 *Catharine Furze*.

1894 A new edition of the translation of Spinoza's *Ethic*, with a long Introduction.

1895 Translation from the Latin of Spinoza's *Tractatus de Intellectus Emendatione*. Read his paper, "The Wilsonian Theory of Sunspots," before the British Astronomical Association, in whose *Journal* it was then published.

1896 *Clara Hopgood*; attacked as immoral. "Spinoza's Doctrine of the Relationship Between Mind and Body" in *The International Journal of Ethics*.

1897 *Description of the Wordsworth and Coleridge Manuscripts in the Possession of Mr. T. Norton Longman*, edited with notes, published. *The Inner Life of Commons*, by William White, with an Introduction by Hale White, published.

1898 *An Examination of the Charge of Apostasy Against Wordsworth*.

## Chronology

1899   Traced the letters of Dorothy Wordsworth to Mrs. Arthur Tennyson, widow of Lord Tennyson's brother. *Coleridge's Poems, a Facsimile Reproduction of the Proofs and MSS. of Some of the Poems*, with preface and notes. Visited the Wordsworth and Coleridge country in the Quantocks.

1900   *Pages from a Journal.*

1901   Letters on the astronomy of Tolstoy, Carlyle, Tennyson, and Coleridge in various journals in this and the following year.

1902   "George Eliot as I Knew Her" in *The Bookman.*

1903   Moved to Groombridge, the home of his last years.

1904   Selections from the letters of Dorothy Wordsworth, edited by Hale White, published in *The Athenaeum.*

1905   *John Bunyan* (a biography).

1907   *Selections from Dr. Johnson's "Rambler,"* edited with preface and notes. A new edition of Carlyle's *The Life of John Sterling*, with an introduction by Hale White. Met and fell in love with Dorothy Vernon Horace Smith, then thirty-one.

1910   *More Pages from a Journal.* "Faith," a short story, in *The Nation.* Contributed numerous articles to *The Nation* during this period, most of them collected later in *Last Pages from a Journal.*

1911   Married Dorothy Vernon Horace Smith.

1913   Died on March 14 at Groombridge. *The Early Life of Mark Rutherford.*

1915   *Last Pages from a Journal.*

1924   *Letters to Three Friends.* Dorothy Vernon White's *The Groombridge Diary*, a record of Hale White's life with her.

*Mark Rutherford*
*(William Hale White)*

## CHAPTER 1

# *The Man and the Novels*

THERE is a strain of quiet but enterprising sensibility in the nineteenth century that is common to authors as varied as Matthew Arnold, Gerard Manley Hopkins, Francis Kilvert, Emily Dickinson, and Henry David Thoreau. Not "Victorian" in the vulgar sense, their work is marked by the kind of poignant awareness that distinguishes both the poetic and the religious experience, as well as by a tact that shuns effusiveness or sentimentality. To this group of authors belongs William Hale White.

Better known under his pseudonym "Mark Rutherford," Hale White reflects from many angles the interests and tastes of the Victorian man of sensibility. His curious mind touched upon most of the nineteenth-century compromises, in politics and philosophy, in science and religion, and in fiction and literary criticism. And it touched upon them always with a certain fervor, discriminating and intense. His novels, too, are marked by this quality. They remain indeed the single clear echo of an extremely powerful and rather small segment of English culture—the Calvinistic minority that reached back to Oliver Cromwell and to John Bunyan and that had, one suspects, a determining influence on the Victorian milieu.

The life of Hale White (1831-1913), overlapping Victoria's long reign, has its own interest for anyone concerned with the sources of human creativeness. It is a story of an almost incredible late flowering. After a boyhood of country freedom and a youthful experience of rebirth, Hale White was throughout the years of his prime imprisoned in a continuous routine of drudgery. His day began typically before dawn, to provide an hour or so for meditation and study. From then on it was a treadmill: a regular office job at Whitehall, an evening reporting job at the House of Commons, an ensuing nightly chore of composing his "London Letter" on the House debates for various provincial journals. This was extra work he took on to eke out enough for his large family and his hopelessly ill wife. The letters had to be ready by Thursday for publication on Saturday every week for twenty-two years. Yet as soon as the pressure lessened, when he was about fifty, he blossomed almost miraculously into a gifted writer. He flourished thereafter for over three decades, until his death at the age of eighty-one.

The sources for this phenomenal old age lay deep within Hale White's personality. They are discernible intermittently in all his writings and are disclosed circumstantially, under a protective veil of fiction, in his first two autobiographical novels.

## I  *Seriousness*

A sense of seriousness, compounded of a Calvinistic search for salvation and a Victorian search for truth, underlies all Hale White's work. It determines the distinctive tone of his masterpieces, *The Autobiography of Mark Rutherford* and *The Revolution in Tanner's Lane*. Hale White never descends to the trivial. The search was always going on within him. To Miss Dorothy Vernon Smith, whom he married at the age of eighty, he remarked, " 'You are the only person who does not mind my being serious. I can't *help* being serious.' "[1]

The search started in his youth, after his awakening under the influence of the *Lyrical Ballads*. "Of more importance, too," he notes of this influence, "than the decay of systems was the birth of a habit of inner reference and a dislike to occupy myself with anything which did not in some way or other touch the soul, or was not the illustration or embodiment of some spiritual law."[2] From this time onward he felt that there was some destiny he had to fulfill. "I have a strange fancy—that there is one word which I was sent into the world to say. At times I can dimly make it out but I cannot speak it. Nevertheless it seems to make all other speech beside the mark and futile."[3] But he had not a hint of self-importance. He realized the tendency to self-deception in all human nature, especially his own. "It is curious that I always have such a sense of insincerity when I try to speak on solemn subjects, even when I do my best to say what I mean and no more than what I mean."[4]

He pounced on superficiality at once. A book for him, if it was anything at all, was the essence of a life—to be cultivated as part of a spacious domain. For this reason he arose habitually between five and six every morning to read and write. This was the only portion of a heavily chartered day he could afford for his central vocation. (Even during his last years, after he retired, his wife reports of him, "when I woke it was generally to find him with a volume of Shakespeare or Spenser or a book from the London library in his hand.")[5] Superficiality in people repelled him in the same way. "Never try to say anything remarkable," he advises. "It is sure to be wrong."[6] He approached his friends as devoutly as he did his books. "For what do my friends stand? Not for the clever things they say: I do not remember them half an hour after they are spoken. It is always the unspoken, the unconscious which is their reality to me."[7]

## II  *Melancholy*

Hale White's attitudes had a discoverable basis. Through his life we can observe a vein of melancholia, sometimes verging on hypochondria, which helped to color his serious cast of thought. "Hypochondrial misery," he notes, "is apt to take an intellectual shape. The most hopeless metaphysics or theology which we happen to encounter fastens on us, and we mistake for an unbiased conviction the form which the disease assumes."[8] This analysis of Wordsworth's Godwinian period bears the note of personal involvement. The experience was projected as Mark Rutherford's own in the *Autobiography*, where "the main curse of my existence has not been pain or loss, but gloom; the blind wandering in a world of black fog, haunted by apparitions."[9] The "depression and *ennui*" which Matthew Arnold in his opening lecture as Professor of Poetry at Oxford singled out as characteristic of "the representative works of modern times," the *mal de siècle* that infects Werther and Childe Harold and Teufelsdröckh, that puts its mark on James Thompson and Hardy and Gissing, becomes for Hale White focused as a special and lifelong blight.

His first bout with such suffering occurred on the eve of his first job as a school teacher. When, after a supper alone in the empty classroom, he had climbed up a ladder to his tiny room at Stoke Newington, looked out at the lonely distance to London, and pondered the dull glare of its lights, "there fell upon me," he records in his memoir of his own early life, "what was the beginning of a trouble that has lasted all my life."[10] In later years it recurred with increased intensity. At the age of seventy-seven he writes: "This nervous disorder is exactly, in reality, what I had to endure many years ago and I hoped it would never recur."[11] The nervous disorder was accompanied in his later years (and all his writings come from those years) by horrible nightmares, indigestion, and general wretchedness.[12] Much of this distress is voiced through Mark Rutherford, in whom the disease breeds a feeling of separateness from his fellow men: "Of all the dreadful trials which human nature has to bear unshattered, the worst . . . is the fang of some monomaniacal idea which cannot be wrenched out. A main part of the misery . . . lies in the belief that suffering of this kind is peculiar to ourselves. We are afraid to speak of it, and not knowing therefore, how common it is, we are distracted with the fear that it is our especial disease."[13] Here we may observe something of that fear of not being understood, which is connected with his inordinate shyness and reticence. In such experiences of suffering and in the consequent self-analysis, he gained the sympathetic knowledge of human nature which his fiction reveals.

However, this melancholia did not vanquish him; it is the only aberration in an unusually energetic life. It cannot be easily forgotten that at the age of eighty Hale White still felt young and hopeful enough to get married.[14] The future Mrs. White pictures him at the age of seventy-seven: "He sprang into this hansom with the three volumes, the DeMorgan titles and his umbrella under his arm. His activity and promptitude are marvelous."[15] Or again, at seventy-four, when rain would be a dangerous thing: "I went out in the worst of tempests," he writes a friend, "to see once more the Medway swirling under the stone arches of old Hendal Bridge. I cannot remember that I ever had to face rain in such masses and with such violence. But oh! how I did enjoy it! Wasn't it sweet?"[16] There were two sides to the life of the man, and both were necessary for his work.

### III  *Reticence*

A related feature which strikes us as curious, almost unique, is Hale White's extreme reticence about his writing, especially in view of the utter frankness with which he wrote. "He is very vague about what he has done," Mrs. White says, "and very apologetic. He much regrets that his authorship was ever known."[17] Invariably this attitude crops up in the course of his life whenever reference is made to his books. "According to Molly" (his only daughter), we again learn from Mrs. White, "if they are mentioned, he turns his back and says, 'I acknowledge no books.' "[18] To protect himself this "most secretive of authors," as M. Louis Cazamian calls him,[19] hid under two pseudonyms ("Mark Rutherford," as edited by his friend, "Reuben Shapcott"). He exploited a convention of the Victorian confessional novel for his own purposes of complete withdrawal from public recognition. This attitude made him, says Mrs. White, "delightfully unprofessional"; he averred "most emphatically," she goes on, "that he was never in the literary world; not educated for literature; he has known hardly any literary people."[20] Story writing, as a matter of fact, was somehow not quite becoming. "I wish I had never written stories. They are somewhat of a degradation."[21] It may have been this sense of "degradation," coupled with his occasional feeling of the uselessness of literature in general, and also his extreme humility, that determined the odd manner he adopted on this one matter in regard to everybody. "Even to me he speaks of them," says Mrs. White, referring to his books, "in an odd unaccustomed way, and not as if he had written them. He said 'you will find in that book Miriam's schooling,' etc., etc. . . ."[22] Even to his intimates, who knew all about his work, he was reserved.

One effect of this reserve was the loss of the society "of all the interesting people in England" who might have lightened his days and replaced "much that is ugly, monotonous and depressing." Notable among such people was George Eliot, one of his first London friends, and co-worker at Chapman's. "It is a lasting sorrow to me," he remarked later in life, "that I allowed my friendship with her to drop, and that after I left Chapman I never called on her." There were others too. "The curse for me," says his narrator in "Confessions of a Self Tormentor," "has not been plucking forbidden fruit, but the refusal of divine fruit offered me by heavenly angels."[23] Allied with this shyness is a humility which, when we consider the abilities and accomplishments of the man, carries traces of the Calvinistic sense of sin from his inherited and rejected religion. "Then he spoke of the sense of 'unworthiness' which always oppressed him,"[24] Mrs. White notes.

## IV  *Sensitivity to Beauty*

Behind the barrier of Hale White's reticence lay not only a warm heart but a keen eye and ear. He responded to the faintest touch of delicacy or beauty. Even neatness of dress or a carefully tended hand gave him pleasure: "delicate hands and feet," says Mark Rutherford, "with delicate care bestowed thereon, were more attractive to me than slovenly beauty."[25] Confined as his life was by unremitting and dull work, he longed for the freedom and the rewarding discipline of beauty. "If I had my life over again," he writes to Miss Dorothy Smith, "I would perpetually urge and strengthen myself to admire and lose myself in pure beauty. I would teach myself to *worship* the beauty of the autumn, the skies, the sea. This worship needs discipline. . . . I would give myself up more systematically to beauty than to reason; make the study of beauty my business."[26]

Whenever he could escape from London to the countryside he became exuberant as a boy. The sky especially delighted him with its panoramic shifts of cloud and color. "This sunset," he says in a random note, "which is common to the whole country, is more to me than anything exclusively mine."[27] It was nature that, through Wordsworth, had first awakened in him a sense of the universe and a religion of his own. With painstaking accuracy he put down what he saw there in the "plain-glass style" which he had learned from his father and from the Bible. In note after note his words echo the form they transcribe: "It is the very summit of the year, the brief poise of perfection. In two or three weeks the days will be noticeably shorter, the harvest will begin, and we shall be on our way downwards to autumn, to dying leaves and to winter."[28] His descriptions are exercises in restraint. Here, perhaps more than anywhere else, does his artistic skill impress us, because here some effusiveness might be overlooked in view of the romantic proclivities of his time. His feeling carries directly over to us through a transparent medium.

Both painting and music delighted him. As a child he had wanted to become a painter; his father's refusal had been one of his early disappointments.[29] In his notebooks he tried to fix in words his sharp impressions of sky and landscape. "How singularly beautiful," he observes for instance, "is a definitely outlined white cloud when it is out by the ridge of a hill!" Or apropos of Dorothy Wordsworth's ability to be absorbed by "pure beauty" without the intrusion of philosophical speculation, he asks, "For how long can we watch a birch tree against the sky?"[30]

Although he rarely assumes the role of critic, references to art exhibits are frequent in his letters. He was acquainted with not a few of the painters of his day. Among his friends were Ruskin, D. G. Rossetti, Millais, Fred Walker, Arthur Hughes, the Burne-Joneses, and William Morris (whose "most effectual service," he believed, lay not in his writing but in his art work).[31] The painting of the Pre-Raphaelites seems particularly to have attracted him. "Their Pre-Raphaelite beauty," he says of some water colors by Boyce, "is enough to break your heart with ecstasy."[32] He wrote a warm review of Holman Hunt's *Isabella and the Pot of Basil*.[33] Of all contemporary painters, however, he gave Millais top rank. "To me," he says of Millais' imagination, "he is the only painter who has any that is healthy, the only one who can seize a dramatic position, whose pictures have a point."[34]

His tastes in music reveal a naturally discriminating and highly developed ear. They are strictly conservative; the genuinely "classical" music delights him most. He damns Wagner for "setting metaphysical problems to music."[35] His enthusiasm is for Bach, Mozart, Beethoven—and Chopin. It was this music that Mrs. White played for him at Groombridge, the home of his later years. "Bach has a strange power over me," he writes. "I suppose something has happened to me articulately inexpressible, which he accompanies."[36] Mozart also, we learn, "has always been one of my divinities." "'Divine' is really the right word for such celestial melodies. Heaven's High King does not, I am sure, lend his ear to more rapturous music."[37] Then Mrs. White tells us of how on one occasion he "raved" about Beethoven; and George Eliot found, as Hale White himself confided to Sir William Robertson Nicoll, "a sure passport to his heart" by frequently playing that composer to him.[38] "Music," Mrs. White again tells us, "excites him just like poetry."[39]

In fine, what he says of his father in his introduction to a collection of the elder White's parliamentary sketches might on every point be applied with equal force to himself: "underneath the simplicity and directness which externally were his most obvious characteristics, there lay imagination and a singular capacity for being moved by that which is genuinely sublime in nature and art."[40]

Notwithstanding this capacity, it must not be supposed that Hale White loses himself for very long in esthetic flights or "escapes." He seemed weighted to earth by his moralistic, Puritan background. Beauty for him is not sufficient in itself, but it is justified upon a moral ground—not that it must be superficially coupled with a "message." Hale White is more subtle than that. He rather indicates an identification of the esthetic and the moral. His thinking on this point is often quite close to that of Ruskin (himself a disciple of Carlyle), for whom good taste was essentially a moral quality, and art an expression of character. ("Tell me what you like," Ruskin had said, "and I'll tell you what you are.")[41] Hale White's criticism of *Paradise Regained* may be cited here as an example of this Victorian "moral aesthetic." This poem, which for him reaches the zenith of art, serves a moral function, he emphasizes, by means of its esthetic qualities. "It is just the most perfect bit of expression ever achieved by man, and do not let us think that perfection of expression is a mere luxury. It is *morality*."[42]

In another place, Hale White stresses the necessity for a life of cleanness and virtue for a true appreciation of beauty as not only Ruskin did, but as the great predecessor of both in the Puritan tradition, John Milton, had done. Only a man whose character is pure can respond with the force of all his faculties to a thing of beauty. In *Catharine Furze* Hale White makes the leading male character, the Reverend Mr. Cardew, observe that "the love of the beautiful cannot long exist where there is moral pollution. The love of the beautiful itself is moral—that is to say, what we love in it is virtue. A perfect form or a delicate colour are the expression of something which is destroyed in us by subjection to the baser desires or meanness, and he who has been unjust to man or woman misses the true interpretation of a cloud or falling wave."[43]

### V *"Puritanism"*

Concerning this devotion to beauty in nature and in art, we can observe a definite ascetic element in Hale White's nature. Passion is always something to be kept at a distance. It is usually

## The Man and the Novels

a "baser desire." It does not interest him as material for literature; he tries to modulate it in his own writings. "Passion," he says, "is considered to be interesting, and the more interesting the less it is under control, but in peace and subjugation real interest also lies."[44] He is capable of saying, in phrases which place him in a world so remote from our own, "To this day I do not know where to find a weapon strong enough to subdue the tendency to impurity in young men; and although I cannot tell them what I do not believe, I hanker sometimes after the old prohibitions and penalties."[45]

Although women are prominent in his fiction, becoming indeed the protagonists of his later novels, his interest is in them as characters of a definitely circumscribed type, the ideal of the Christian (and Pre-Raphaelite) tradition—saintly, otherworldly, and above all self-controlled. In his description of a picture of a nineteen-year-old girl he discloses that "The body was shown down to the waist, and was slim and graceful. But what was most noteworthy about the picture was its solemn seriousness, a seriousness capable of infinite affection, and of infinite abandonment, no sensuous abandonment—everything was too severe, too much controlled by the arch of the top of the head for that—but of an abandonment to spiritual aims."[46] The dichotomy here between the sensuous and the spiritual, the injunction to control the one and abandon oneself to the other, partly excuses Mr. Massingham's remark about Hale White: "But once a Puritan, always a Puritan."[47]

Yet, concerning Hale White's "Puritanism," two observations can be made. One is that the sentiments expressed in his writings are always those of a man past the meridian of his life. "Youth with its heat in the blood may be more capable of exultation," he observes of his happiness of a fine April day, "but to the old man it brings the sounder hope and deeper joy."[48] Furthermore, nothing is ever quite simple in a sensibility so refined as that of Hale White. "Once a Puritan always a Puritan" is in fact no truer of him than it was of Milton. It he values discipline, he also revels in wildness and disorder. Some of the harshest judgments in his novels are reserved for men who become the slaves of daily routine and women whose compulsive insistence on order in their homes kills the feeling of home itself. In contrast, the sprawling, semi-wild gardens; the straggling, sportive orchards; the slow, grand river of his Bedfordshire boyhood; and, even more, its ample kitchens and cluttered, cozy parlors all keep returning to him as touchstones for a human way of living.

It is not for nothing that Wordsworth replaced Calvin as Hale White's guide, or that Spinoza's unification of all nature appealed to him as a corrective to the Puritan dualism of good and evil, of "higher" and "lower" faculties in man. His ambivalence with regard to Puritanism emerges clearly in the very last sentences of his book on John Bunyan. After celebrating for pages the Puritan and Kantian distinction between right and wrong, he remarks that "it is not an entirely accurate version of God's message to men." No other religion has surpassed Puritanism, he says, "in preaching the truths by which men and nations must exist. Nevertheless we need Shakespeare as well as Bunyan." He concludes with a plea for a unity that surmounts the old dichotomy between good and evil in man: "We cannot bring ourselves into a unity. The time is yet to come when we shall live by a faith which is a harmony of all our faculties. A glimpse was caught of such a gospel nineteen centuries ago in Galilee, but it has vanished."[49]

The ideal women of Hale White's novels embody such a harmony. His favorite image for them is that of a wild bird among the barnyard fowls. Characteristically they have in their blood and in their names a touch of French (Pauline Caillaud, Miss Leroy)—that vigorous symbol of permissiveness in Victorian England. It is for her superiority to convention that Hale White also loved George Eliot—for her "Insurgent" nature. The heroes and heroines of his novels are fiercely honest, alien to the Puritan religiosity of the petty lives around them.

## VI  *Iconoclasm*

Hale White likes to smash idols. In this respect, as in so many others, he resembles Carlyle. He has the independence that will proclaim that the emperor wears no clothes. His cry for honesty reaches down to us as a late-ninteenth-century echo. Even honesty with an eccentric twist is something, as long as it saves us from dullness and stupidity. "There isn't a democrat, socialist, doubter, or disciple of any ism from the railway station to the Beacon Road," he writes of his home in the town of Crowborough, "and at times I feel as if I could welcome a Theosophist, or anti-vaccinationist or even the American lady who has just discovered Bacon was the son of Elizabeth by Leicester."[50]

This rebelliousness, spreading so quickly among the younger men around him, shows what was happening to him and to his age, and had indeed been happening to him all his life—the tremendous crumbling of the distinctive Victorian certainties. Respectability, the Victorian middle way, is by its nature opposed to integrity; and is, in fact, a kind of evil: "For respectability is really the devil, imposture, lying, thieving, the root of evil."[51] In simplicity he sees truth. "He likes," Mrs. White notes, "to be with simple people and talk about simple things."[52] He complains of how such truth has been perverted in the dressed-up biography of George Eliot that her husband, J. W. Cross, has published. "I think he has made her too 'respectable,'" he writes in a letter of protest to the *Athenaeum*. "She was really one of the most sceptical, unusual creatures I ever knew, and it was this side of her character which to me was the most attractive. . . . I confess I hardly recognize her in the pages of Mr. Cross's . . . volumes."[53]

In the life of the mind his rejection of pretense is special and violent. Here the moral bias cannot be separated from the intellectual. It stems from a sharp sagacity that sees through counterfeits. It leads, among other things, to a scorn for bookishness. For himself, he was living out all his life a bit of advice given to him by Carlyle in that moralist's eloquent manner when he was young. "If my books teach you anything," Carlyle had written to him, "don't mind in the least whether other people believe it or not; but do you for your own behoof lay it to heart as a real acquisition you have made, more properly as a real message left with you, which *you* must set about fulfilling, whatsoever others do! This is really all the counsel I can give you about what you read in my works or those of others: *practice* what you learn there, instantly and in all ways begin turning the belief into a fact. . . . It is idle work otherwise to write books or to read them."[54]

Theories, likewise, are not in themselves significant for him. "What we believe is not of so much importance as the path by which we travel to it." Ideas which alone count are those which yield a profit by "turning the belief into a fact." "There is but little thinking, or perhaps it is correct to say but little reflection in the Bible. There is profound sympathy with a few truths, but ideas are not sought for their own sake. Carlyle is Biblical. It has been said scoffingly that he is no thinker. It is his glory that he is not."[55]

At work here is Romantic anti-intellectualism. Frequently in the course of his life he felt the bitter contrast between the wisdom attributed to the great books and their inadequacy during periods of actual suffering and need. Clara Hopgood, the perspicaceous heroine of his last novel, realizes this: "Whenever Mrs. Caffyn talked about the labourers of Great Oakhurst, whom she knew so well, Clara always felt as if all her reading had been a farce, and, indeed, if we come into close contact with actual life, art, poetry and philosophy seem little better than trifling."[56] The same point is made in connection with his first heroine, Miriam, who has read absolutely nothing. In her greatest misery, "she was spared . . . that savage disappointment to which many are doomed who in their trouble find that all philosophy fails them, and the books on their shelves look so impotent, so beside the mark, that they narrowly escape being pitched into the fire."[57]

Hale White attacks both literature and philosophy because he loves them so much. Actually, it is their desecration that he indicts. No one could be a more careful scholar than he, as his work on the Wordsworth and Coleridge manuscripts shows. "He said that he should like to have his life over again and go in for Greek research,"[58] Mrs. White tells us, for example. He charges so furiously against the fraudulent because he identifies so passionately with the authentic. From the vantage which the habits of a long life allow him, he shrewdly perceives the abuses to which these habits are liable, abuses which interfere with the sources of experience or its flow, or else pollute its freshness—literature confined to books, philosophy confined to systems (Bacon's Idol of the Theatre), and beyond those, religion in the guise of religiosity, manners in the guise of the "genteel."

No summary could do justice to the antinomies in Hale White's personality—his learning and his anti-intellectualism, his melancholy and his vitality, his asceticism and his estheticism, his sense of discipline and his delight in disorder, his idealism and his iconoclasm. He is not quite like any of the better known

## The Man and the Novels

Victorians, though almost any one of his traits in isolation may remind us of one or another of them—the elegiac seriousness of Matthew Arnold, for example; the rugged, practical streak and the moral ardor of Carlyle; the passion for pure beauty of Keats and the Pre-Raphaelites; the bias against abstractness and pretentiousness in favor of the blunt, the vital, and the lowly of both Wordsworth and Dickens. It is this original and universal nature that makes Hale White unique and a representative Victorian.

### VII  *The World of the Novels*

In an age of three-decker novels, the slim volumes of Hale White, critical, searching, and unadorned, stand apart. An anonymous reviewer of *The Autobiography of Mark Rutherford* said just after its publication, "It is remarkable. It is short and that in itself is a merit in these days of weary three volumes."[59] Hale White's first two novels crossed the Atlantic and were reviewed by William Dean Howells in *Harper's New Monthly Magazine*; he immediately recognized their distinction:

There never were books [said Howells] in which apparently the writer has cared so little to make literary account of himself, cared so little to shine, to impress, wished so much to speak his heart plainly out to the heart of his reader. There is absolutely no study of attitudes, no appeal to the dramatic or the picturesque, no merely decorative use of words. When you have read the books you feel you have witnessed the career of a man as you might have witnessed it in the world, and not in a book. We could not give too strong an impression of their incomparable sincerity.[60]

The locale of these novels, when it is not London, is typically a small English market town like Hale White's native Bedford on the meadow flats of the eastern midlands. In the opening chapter of *Catharine Furze*, which of all his novels recaptures most lovingly the country of his boyhood, the scene is given in a single encompassing sentence:

The malthouses and their cowls, the wharves and the gaily painted sailing barges alongside, the fringe of slanting willows turning the silver-gray sides of their foliage towards the breeze, the island in the middle of the river with bigger willows, the large expanse of sky, the soft clouds distinct in form almost to the far distant horizon, and, looking eastwards, the illimitable distance towards the fens and the sea—all this made up a landscape, more suitable perhaps to some persons than rock or waterfall, although no picture had ever been painted of it and nobody had ever come to see it.

Actually, this is the charming countryside we are shown in John Constable's paintings. This land of meadow and wood and river, of farm and mill and wharf had been the scene of Constable's own Suffolk childhood in the valley of the river Stour, which separates that county on the south from Essex. These counties occupy those very fenlands stretching eastward from Bedford and Cambridge to the sea. These "scenes of his boyhood," Constable had been fond of saying, "made him a painter." He had celebrated them on his canvases during the first four decades of the century, decades which included Hale White's own boyhood. In Constable's pictures we are given the landscape of Hale White's "Cowfolds." Hale White pays his tribute to those "fields by the banks of the Stour." "It is Constable's country," he says in his *Early Life*, "and in its way not to be matched in England. Although there is nothing striking in it, its influence, at least upon me, is greater than that of celebrated mountains and waterfalls."[61]

All Hale White's characters are taken from his own life in a sense more literal than is true for most novelists. "He never created a character in his life," his wife records, "never sat down to write without having somebody before his mind's eye."[62] These novels, written in his fifties and sixties, in the London of the 1880's and 1890's, re-create the rural countryside of the early decades of the century—a world that has all but disappeared: the River Ouse with its bridges and barges, the spicy talk of the farmers drinking whiskey in back parlors, the bustle and anger of politics—Chartism, Reform—against the still vivid memory of the French Revolution.

Hale White's world is one that has not altogether found a place in the great novels. It is not quite the circle of *Adam Bede*, nor at all that of *Barchester Towers*, nor of *The Way of All Flesh*. Thackeray was not aware of it, and Dickens merely caricatured it. It is the world which Hale White himself came from and which he knew best. "I seem to have come from an honest set," he writes to his future wife, "but socially nothing much above farmers who may have been and indeed very likely were officers

## The Man and the Novels

in Oliver's army.[63] Their forebears were the Saxons, who having in the fourteenth century been driven to the towns by the Black Death, had become merchants and developed a vigorously independent style of life. Their religion was simple, with none of the ornateness that flourished among the Norman feudal lords and that was later to develop into "Anglicanism." From this Saxon tradition of the fenlands came—together with Bunyan and Cromwell's soldiers—the shopkeepers, ironmongers, brewers, printers, and booksellers of Hale White's novels, a working class homely of speech, of manner, and of religion, independent, and, when occasion demanded, rebellious of thought and temper. To this world Hale White restricts himself in his novels, and by so doing becomes its principal spokesman. "He is by his own right," William Learoyd Sperry delimits it finely, "the spokesman for mid-Victorian Independency, a world which without his witness would have been mute and perhaps ultimately forgotten. He has done for the humble nonconformity of his own midland counties what Trollope did for the Establishment in sleepy Cathedral towns, what George Eliot did for Methodism through the countryside, and what Jane Austen and Miss Mitford did for innocuous gentility at large. 'Cowfold' is the 'Barchester' of Dissent."[64]

Hale White's milieu is as far removed from Barchester as Barchester is from London. His "Cowfolds" are, as he puts it in the *Autobiography*, "a sort of condensation of the agricultural country round."[65] Like Gray's *Elegy*, Hale White's novels celebrate the romance that lies implicit, and that can at times achieve a glory of its own, in the annals of the poor. But these annals for him are not short nor simple. In them lie entangled the very complexities of motive and deed that dominate the courts and capitals of the world.

There were no villains amongst the portion of the inhabitants with which this history principally concerns itself [he says of the Cowfold of his *Revolution*], nor was a single adventure of any kind ever known to happen beyond the adventures of being born, getting married, falling sick, and dying, with now and then an accident from a gig. Consequently it might be thought that there was no romance in Cowfold. There could not be a greater mistake. The history of every boy and girl of ordinary make is one of robbery, murder, imprisonment, death sentence, filing of chains, scaling of prison walls, recapture, scaffold, reprieve, poison, and pistols; the difference between such a history and that in the authorized versions being merely circumstantial. The garden of Eden, the murder of Cain, the deluge, the salvation of Noah, the exodus from Egypt, David and Bathsheba, with the murder of Uriah, the Assyrian invasion, the Incarnation, the Atonement, and the Resurrection from the Dead; to say nothing of the Decline and Fall of the Roman Empire, the tragedy of Count Cenci, the execution of Mary Queen of Scots, the Inquisition in Spain, and Revolt of the Netherlands, all happened in Cowfold, as well as elsewhere, and were perhaps more interesting there because they could be studied in detail and the records were authentic.[66]

It was this "uncovering of the 'commonplace,'" as she phrased it, which first drew Dorothy Vernon Smith, later his second wife, to his books.[67] Hale White himself intimates in one sentence of *Catharine Furze* the meaning of his novels: "When we grow old we find that what is commonplace is true. . . ."[68] With the Romantic bias which was sharpened under the influence of Wordsworth, his purpose is to present the ordinary in an unusual way. "In Wordsworth the miraculous inherent in the commonplace, but obscured by 'the film of familiarity,' is restored to it," he has observed.[69] The discoveries that he embodies in his stories are however his own. The facts which unsettle and propel him are peculiarly urban. His are among the first of the "proletarian" novels. "What are the facts?" he asks in one of his detached notes. "Not those in Homer, Shakespeare or even the Bible. The facts for most of us are a dark street, crowds, hurry commonplaceness, loneliness, and, worse than all, a terrible doubt which can hardly be named as to the meaning and purpose of the world."[70] Nor is it the peasant mentality to which his Romantic inheritance draws him. It is in "second-rate sensitive minds" exposed to the rootlessness of modern life that he is interested.

The protagonists of Hale White's novels are essentially projections of his own youthful temperament. "I wish not to judge others," he says in the *Autobiography* "but the persons who to me have proved themselves most attractive, have been those who have passed through such a process as that through which I myself passed; those who have had in some form or other an enthusiastic stage in their history, when the story of Genesis and the Gospels has been rewritten, when God has visibly walked in the garden, and the Son of God has drawn men away from their daily occupations to the divinest of dreams."[71]

## The Man and the Novels

Hale White combines in a remarkable way strands from the seventeenth century and from the nineteenth. The latter appear in the intellectual conflict of his characters; the former are implicit in their stern, Puritan idealism, which intesifies that conflict. The story of Genesis and the Gospels has been rewritten by his heroes. Hale White's special achievement is to restore to the Christian terminology its original meaning in existential terms. "Nearly every doctrine in the college creed had once had a natural origin in the necessities of human nature, and might therefore be so interpreted as to become a necessity again," says Mark Rutherford in the *Autobiography* during his short career as a theological student. Ironically, he learned that it was just such interpretation, leading back to the origins of creed, that the authorities feared and misunderstood: "To reach through to that original necessity; to explain the atonement as I believed it appeared to Paul, and the sinfulness of man as it appeared to the prophets, was my object. But it was precisely this reaching after a meaning which constituted heresy."

Hale White's theology, as we shall see later, was to develop quickly in the direction of a symbolism which read the old creed in terms of an ever new existence. His novels embody these views and their growth. What must one do to be saved? The answer to this question is the persistent theme of his fiction. In the earlier autobiographical novels—whose protagonist, Mark Rutherford, is Hale White himself "under a semi-transparent disguise"—the metaphysical problem of the age, echoed in poets like Clough and Arnold and Tennyson, is expressed by Hale White in the very specific context of the Calvinistic creed. Mark is torn by the loss of the old belief and relives the words of the twenty-second Psalm, "My God, my God, why hast thou forsaken me?" His need is not for the rationalized deity of the schools but for a personal union. In these earlier novels Hale White has undertaken to show us the disintegration of a religion. Part of his aim is to contrast a fading Puritanism with the fiery ardor of the earlier sect. This ardor is relit in a few isolated souls, like Mark Rutherford and Zachariah Coleman, incarnations of pristine nonconformity in the nineteenth-century muddle. The fading is a symptom of prosperity and middle-class attitudes. Calvinism has climbed almost to the respectability of Anglicanism. It is this climb which evokes the dominant note of irony in the novels.

Hale White's early male protagonists are Job-like heroes of endurance; his later, female protagonists tend to be, like Ibsen's Nora, more rebellious. Hale White's special subject is the predicament of ardent, Christ-like spirits in a prosperous, alien world; his special contribution to English fiction is the rendition, unsentimental and acute, of their endurance. No one equals him in projecting into fiction the stoical lesson which was impressed upon him by Carlyle and which he expresses as follows: "Carlyle feels the contradictions of the universe as keenly as any man can feel them. He knows how easy it is to appear profound by putting anew riddles which nobody can answer; he knows how strong is the temptation toward the insoluable. But upon these subjects he also knows how to hold his tongue; he does not shriek in the streets, but he bows his head."[72]

Gradually, in the later novels, the exigencies of living apply their balm to the pain of youthful frustration. Solutions begin to appear: absorption in work (*Mark Rutherford's Deliverance*), and politics and love (*The Revolution in Tanner's Lane*). The problem is blunted but the ache is still there. It persists through all the later novels under the guise of new circumstance. The most radical alteration in these later novels is, as their titles indicate, that their protagonists are women, and that the change of sex is accompanied by a change in the phrasing of the question. The search for a God becomes a search for a human relationship. It is as though women, with their sense of the practical, can confer another perspective, can view the problem of salvation naturalistically. In these novels the "new woman" of the later nineteenth century (modeled for Hale White in many features by George Eliot) emerges.

For all their concern with the problem of love, these later novels are however not "love stories." They are quite as concentrated as were the earlier novels on the issues of struggle and salvation. This is what distinguishes them, the sense they establish of the dependence of the immediate on the ultimate. They convey a Spinozistic view of the human situation *sub specie aeternitatis*. If they are not love stories, neither are they "religious novels" in any pious sense; they are so only if we interpret religion broadly enough to include a secular non-supernatural humanism.[73] Then they are truly so. They are ever questioning both the dogma and the skepticism of the nineteenth century. Apropos of the "entertainment" provided at the monthly Sunday evening meetings of his congregation during his term as minister, Mark Rutherford comments on the pious books used for the public readings: "I was reduced to that class of literature which of all others I most abominated, and which always seemed to me the most profane,—religious and sectarian gossip, religious novels designed to make religion attractive, and other slip-slop of this kind."[74] Hale White's own approach is quiet and direct.[75] His seriousness is rarely without its touch of irony. His editorial asides, which are frequent, are woven into the fabric of his stories without noticeable shift of tone, and they do not offend. Even the professional sermons of his ministers are convincing, and keep within the narrow bounds of a fiction reader's patience. Thomas Seccombe has observed of these: "He interpolates several sermons into his novels and these are the only sermons we have read for many years."[76]

The personalities of Hale White's protagonists are derived especially from the idols of his youth. Their qualities of sincerity, skepticism, sensitivity, aloofness, and fearlessness are those Hale White inherited from his own father and discovered anew in one or two older friends and in such literary favorites as Carlyle and Byron. Upon Hale White's heroines the influence of George Eliot (who for him was very much a friend before she was an author) is noticeable. His heroes, men like the Reverend Bradshaw in the *Revolution*, are modeled in part upon the old breed of minister that was passing from the scene in Hale White's childhood. One such, the Reverend Samuel Hilliard, had occupied the pulpit of Bunyan Meeting, the chapel at Bedford, in Hale White's childhood. For half a century he had fearlessly maintained the connection between Dissent and political reform that dated back to Cromwell. He was succeeded by the Reverend John Jukes, neo-orthodox and careful in his politics, the type of the sanctimonious, pussyfooting minister, representative of a decadent, mammonized Dissent, who was to be satirized in the Reverend John Broad of the *Revolution*. When Hale White was eighteen, he came under the influence of an eloquent Welsh preacher, Caleb Morris, who more than any other person except his father influenced his life. Recalling one of Morris' sermons he has written: "I can feel even now the force which streamed from him that night, and swept me with it, as if I were a leaf on a river in a flood. . . . I never beheld a man in whom Christianity, or rather Christ, was so vitally inherent."[77]

Such intensities of realization flash out in the protagonists of Hale White's novels. Caleb Morris represented for him the heroic culmination of qualities in his father and in his father's favorite authors, to which as a boy he had learned to respond. Matthew Arnold has described religion as "the power not ourselves that makes for righteousness." Religion, divested of its theology, was for Hale White too essentially a moral power. As such it came to be articulated for him by great literary spokesmen like Carlyle. Carlyle indeed had been the particular idol of his father, whose religion was colored by the fervor and skepticism of the Scotch author much as Hale's was to be colored by the pantheism of Wordsworth. Fervor and skepticism became the distinguishing traits of Hale White's great male characters, Mark Rutherford and Zachariah Coleman. Byron, too, with his scorn for the petty and the vulgar, his flair for the grand possibilities in life, vanquished with his rhetoric both father and son. Standing at his composing desk, the Puritan printer would declaim from memory long passages from Byron to the enthralled young Hale. The father loved poetry of a sublime cast, especially Milton, and Hale White could in his old age remember his reciting passages from "Comus," his special favorite. Pervasively do Hale White's various interests—in religion and politics, in philosophy and science—inform his novels, but from his literary admirations these novels catch their special note.

The kinship among the protagonists of his novels, the literary and personal heroes of his youth, and Hale White himself, has its origins deep within the Victorian conscience and the Victorian temper. Carlyle, Byron, George Eliot, Caleb Morris, William White, Sr., were all products of the religious awakening that marked the opening decades of the century—an awakening that is evident also in Newman, Arnold, and Ruskin, all temperamentally akin to Hale White and all emergent from similar severe Protestant backgrounds. All of them modified the dogma of the old creed but retained its impassioned moral dedication. Protestant in the sense that the early Reformation leaders were, each

## The Man and the Novels

forged from his own experience, which frequently involved a painful "soul crisis," a religion of his own. Hale White's novels record the agonizing and liberating progress of his own personal religion. In so doing they give us an insight into the Victorian moral ferment as it worked its way from the great spokesmen of the age and was filtered through the sensibility of an intensely individual author.

CHAPTER 2

# *Early Life:*
# The Autobiography of Mark Rutherford

IN the *Autobiography of Mark Rutherford*, Hale White's power is at its steadiest. This quality may be due to the book's deeply personal nature. It is his confession of faith, of doubt, and, more, of his struggle to possess either one absolutely without disturbance from the other. The strength of the two forces in Mark Rutherford makes the conflict fierce. On the one side is Mark's inherited Calvinism, an exacting tradition with roots beyond the reach of rational attacks. On the other side is a keenly logical, inquisitive mind, trained by the very tradition it is helping to undermine. Mark Rutherford's development is the history of a part-believer, part-doubter. Beginning as an Independent minister, he passes through stages of Unitarianism to vague theism, and finally to a vague agnosticism.

The curious reticence which led Hale White to secure himself behind his double-barreled anonymity led him also to disclaim deliberately the authorship of this fine book. "I have never owned the book you name," he writes to one of his oldest friends, Mrs. Colenutt, two years after the publication of the *Autobiography*, "and should be quite justified in denying its authorship." And in the same letter he adds: "Tell——, not as a message from me but as one from yourself, that you understand I disclaim it and that he had better not say a word to me about it." His reserve lay in sources deep within him. It is the symptom of a need which nothing in his life ever did requite. Mrs. White tells us: "He spoke of the 'hunger and thirst and need' of his life, 'an infinite need' which neither his books, nor his friends, nor his religion had ever satisfied."[1] Upon all the heroes of his novels Hale White projects this need. It is the foundation of their characters. Aggravated by their sense of being different, being in

*Early Life:* The Autobiography of Mark Rutherford

some way dedicated and therefore unresponsive to the daily satisfactions and comforts their fellows enjoy, it marks them as ultimately alone. In the *Autobiography* there is a moving passage which commemorates, as it were for our time as well as for his own, the modern syndrome of emotional hunger, its frustration, and the ensuing sense of alienation. "The desire for something like sympathy and love almost devoured me. I dwelt on all the instances in poetry and history in which one human being had been bound to another human being, and I reflected that my existence was of no earthly importance to anybody." He tells us how he has been humiliated and repulsed by those he sought out, and he concludes: "I could not altogether lay the blame on myself. God knows that I would have stood against a wall and have been shot for any man or woman whom I loved, as cheerfully as I would have gone to bed, but nobody seemed to wish for such a love, or to know what to do with it. . . . I am now getting old and have altered in many things. The hunger and thirst of those years have abated, or rather, the fire has had ashes heaped on it, so that it is well-nigh extinguished. I have been repulsed into self-reliance and reserve, having learned wisdom by experience; but still I know that the desire has not died, as so many other desires have died, by the natural evolution of age. It has been forcible suppressed, and that is all."[2] So, we may infer, Hale White's reticence developed, especially with regard to these autobiographical novels, in which he bared his soul with all the passion of a lonely man. Through long enforced effort he had learned to separate his private from his public self. His fellow workers in the Admiralty, where thirty years of his life were spent, knew, for example, nothing whatever about his real nature, let alone his literary work. The surface he presented to them was grim and sternly disciplined. One of his subordinates many years after his retirement summed up the impression Hale White conveyed in five words: "He was a hard nut!"[3] The irony of this characterization only indicates how effectively Hale White preserved his public mask.

How far the *Autobiography* and *Deliverance* are novels and how far they are autobiographies is a moot question. Good autobiography, such as this, has doubtlessly some of the qualities of fiction; and it is rather a commonplace that every novel is in a sense autobiographical. This is especially true of all Hale

White's novels; whatever value they have lies in their spiritual disclosure. For this reason the first two, the "autobiographies," take on especial weight; they purport to do nothing other than to make such disclosure. The very organization of these novels, in the best "naturalistic" vein, is biographical rather than fictional. In them there is no attempt at "plot"; there is no sense of that forcing of circumstance to fit a pattern which was a feature of the "well-made" novels of the time. With the inconsequentiality of life itself, the *Autobiography* and the *Deliverance* unfold the passing of years in a man's life. This is what makes for the "honesty and integrity" which André Gide admired in Hale White's novels.

Though certain aspects of what we know of Hale White's own history may at times be scanty, on every page they convey the impression of literal truth that makes biography often so much more fascinating than fiction. They present indeed that "Reality" which Carlyle in his essay, "Biography," had held superior to "Fiction." Luckily, Hale White has to a certain extent provided us with an external measure of the veracity of these two books—in his *Early Life of Mark Rutherford*. Here in "autobiographical notes," written at the age of seventy-eight, what he "now set down is fact."[4] Yet, even here, he found it hard to distinguish literal fact from poetic truth. While in the process of composing the *Early Life*, he wrote to a friend about it: "I am trying to scrape together for the benefit of my children all that I can recollect of my life from my earliest childhood to my marriage. How much is *wahrheit* and how much *dichtung*?"[5] The dividing line between truth and poetry is similarly vague in the *Autobiography*. Concerning what he has recounted about his youth there, he says in the *Early Life*: "A great deal of it has been told before under a semi-transparent disguise, with much added which is entirely fictitious."[6] The *Early Life* will, with the cautions here indicated, provide us with some measure of the *wahrheit* and the *dichtung* of the *Autobiography*.

## I  *The Son*

The *Autobiography* records nothing of one essential *wahrheit* —the close sympathy which existed between Hale White and his father. This again may be taken as part of Hale White's effort to

*Early Life:* The Autobiography of Mark Rutherford

cover his traces and remain anonymous. His father was well known both in Bedford and London. In London he was the Doorkeeper of the House of Commons, closely acquainted with the political notables of his day. In Bedford he had been a well-patronized bookseller, a Sunday School superintendent, a deacon of the Bunyan Meeting (the Independent Chapel founded by Bunyan himself), and an aggressive political spokesman in the liberal camp. At election times he was in the thick of the struggle, especially during the contest of 1832 when he and the Whig Committee were besieged at the Swan Inn by a Tory mob. His house was attacked in this instance, and the cradle of the one-year-old Hale had to be hustled out of the front bedroom so that the baby's head might not be broken by the stones which smashed the windows.[7] Hale White marked this incident as the first public event in his own life.[8] When Hale was twelve years old, William White was the town hero for having, as a trustee of the Bedford Charity School, defeated with his eloquence a movement to close the schools to Dissenters by obliging all the teachers to be members of the Church of England.

Later, when Hale, at the age of twenty, needed help during his own revolt against ecclesiastical tyranny, having been expelled from theological school on the charge of heresy, his father defended him and the cause of free thought with Miltonic fervor in a pamphlet called *To Think, or, Not to Think*. This vigorous defense illuminated for Hale the essential character of his father. "In 1852 he was forty-five years old," he remarks in this connection. "He had not hardened; he was alive, rejecting what was dead, laying hold of what was true to him, and living by it. . . . What he became in 1852 he was substantially to the end of his life."[9] (He lived to the age of seventy-five.) The pamphlet won the commendation of both F. D. Maurice and Charles Kingsley, who wrote the elder White, "Your son ought to thank God for having a father who will stand by him in trouble so manfully and wisely."[10] By nature, William White was affectionate, merry, and sociable. In London he was always making new friends. His little office, or "sanctum," in the House became what a fellow journalist described as "a favourite resort of choice spirits of whom he was the choicest."[11]

In the *Early Life* Hale White manifests his admiration for his father. He there reveals the affinities which shaped his own

[ 45 ]

character, his politics, and his art: "There was one endowment for which he was remarkable," he says of his father, "the purity of the English he spoke and wrote. He used to say he owed it to Cobbett, whose style he certainly admired, but this is but partly true. It was rather a natural consequence of the clearness of his own mind and of his desire to make himself wholly understood, both demanding the simplest and most forcible expression." From his father, Hale White drew strength to the end of his life. When he was over eighty, he could say of the portrait of the elder White that was always before him in his study, "It helps me and decides me when I look at it."[12]

In the *Autobiography* we get a glimpse of Hale White as a sensitive but friendly child in the midst of a world just on the point of disappearing, of a society primitive in the rigidities of its religion. Life for him in those days separated itself into two distinct parts—weekdays and Sunday. Weekdays, as far as school went, he "learned little or nothing that did me much good," but the half holidays on Wednesdays and Saturdays he remembered as the happiest days in his life. In summer he wandered with his friends for miles along the "sacred" Ouse, fishing and swimming. The Liverpool and Manchester Railway had not yet opened; fifty years later when he wrote the *Autobiography*, hardly a trace, he tells us, was left of the pre-industrial town he had known. "I remember whole afternoons in June, July, and August," he recalls

passed half-naked or altogether naked in the solitary meadows and in the water; I remember the tumbling weir with the deep pool where we dived; I remember, too, the place where we used to swim across the river with our clothes on our heads, because there was no bridge near, and the frequent disaster of a slip of the braces in the middle of the water, so that shirt, jacket, and trousers were soaked, and we had to lie on the grass in the broiling sun without a rag on us till everything was dry again. In winter our joys were of a different kind, but none the less delightful. If it was a frost, we had skating; not like the skating on a London pond, but over long reaches, and if the locks had not intervened, we might have gone a day's journey on the ice without a stoppage. If there was no ice we had football, and what was still better, we could get up a steeple chase on foot straight across Ledge and ditch.[13]

*Early Life:* The Autobiography of Mark Rutherford

Such "perfect poetic pleasures," which flare up brilliantly in his later writing, underlay the signal experience of his youth, his religious awakening under the influence of the *Lyrical Ballads*.

## II "*Religion*"

On Sunday retribution came. The Sabbath was a day of sacredness. Every preparation was made in advance to avoid secular contacts. "The meat was cooked beforehand so that we never had a hot dinner even in the coldest weather." There were three chapel services besides intermittent prayer meetings. Of these only the most unpleasant memories seem to have remained with Hale White. The prayer "was a horrible hypocrisy" which began with a confession of the sinfulness of man, and then "ensued a kind of dialogue with God, very much resembling the speeches which in later years I have heard in the House of Commons from the movers and seconders of addresses to the Crown at the opening of Parliament."[14] But the evening service was the most trying. The boy could not keep awake, yet there was always the overhanging threat that to sleep during the Gospel was a sin. He used to envy the old man who during the middle of the service snuffed the candles on the immense chandeliers. The atmosphere, moreover, was foul. A concern for ventilation was, notoriously, not one of the prepossessions of the early Victorians. In wintertime "the windows streamed with condensed breath, and the air we took into our lungs was poisonous. Almost every Sunday some woman was carried out fainting." Ruskin in his *Praeterita* records similar unpleasant memories from his Evangelical childhood; for him "the horror of Sunday used to cast its prescient gloom as far back in the week as Friday."[15]

Although other factors may have been influential, there may even be some psychological connection between these early unpleasant experiences of Hale White and his later marked disinclination toward the established forms of religion in general. At any rate, Sunday ever afterward remained to him one of the unpleasant necessities of life. Even at the age of sixty-two he wrote to a friend: "Sunday is a day on which I cannot endure gloom; in fact I never care much for Sundays and am glad when they depart."[16] One happy memory he did retain of Sundays, that of going along with his father, who, as a lay preacher, "supplied" the village chapels around Bedford. On these expeditions Hale absorbed much that was later to be turned into his novels—impressions of farmer and preacher, of cottage and church, of the great meadow land and the sacred river.

At sixteen, before going to college, Hale underwent "conversion." In his community this was a sort of initiation rite in the process of which the candidate became a "changed character." Somehow he had to become "a child of God," and in due course Hale professed himself to be one. Then in order to be "admitted" to membership in his church, he had to make a confession of his faith: "As may be expected, it is very often inaccurately picturesque, and is framed after the model of the journey to Damascus."[17] It was part of the ritual to demand of each candidate a description of his "experience." Since he could give none, he was excused on the ground that he was the child of pious parents. Edmund Gosse has given us in his *Father and Son* a similar picture of a sham conversion among Dissenters, as well as of their narrowness and intolerance.[18]

Hale White cannot recall, he says, that after the ceremony he was anything else than he had ever been except that he was perhaps a little bit more hypocritical. "I can see myself now ... stepping out of the pew, standing in the aisle at the pew door and protesting to their content before the minister of the church, father and mother protesting also to my own complete content, that the witness of God in me to my own salvation was as clear as noonday. Poor little mortal, a twelvemonth out of round jackets, I did not in the least know who God was, or what was salvation."[19] Yet embedded in his mind was the theme that Hale White was to pursue through all his novels: salvation in terms much revised, it is true, from those of the old creed, involving searing "experiences" of the soul and recurring frequently to the archetypal image of Paul on the road to Damascus.

### III  *Wordsworth and the Seminary*

At this point came "the great blunder" of his life, as he calls it, "the mistake which well-nigh ruined it altogether."[20] He would like to have gone to Oxford, but the Test Act, barring nonconformists, made this impossible. He would like also to have studied art, but his parents vetoed this. He had to prepare him-

*Early Life:* The Autobiography of Mark Rutherford

self for some vocation, and his mother's desire to have him become a minister won out. His mother was, as he somewhat dryly puts it, a little weak in her preference for people who did not stand behind counters. He was accordingly sent in the fall of 1848, when he was almost seventeen, to a seminary in Hertfordshire, the Countess of Huntington's College at Cheshunt, of which he says he has nothing particular to record except that he learned nothing there and did not make a single friend.

Though he learned nothing at college, he was rapidly developing by himself the aristocratic spirit of his later life. During this period the turning point in this development occurred. Hale White offers an interesting parallel to John Stuart Mill, who records in his *Autobiography* how as a youth he gradually emerged from a period of listlessness and depression under the "healing power" of Wordsworth. Like Mill, Hale White was during this period spiritually deadened, in his case by the aridity of theology; whereas Mill's suffering was due to the aridity of rationalism, which had turned him into "a mere reasoning machine." Again, like Mill, Hale White during this period of negativism, without any goal in life or interest in his theological studies, certainly without any positive religion, suddenly discovered Wordsworth. One day when he happened to pick up a copy of the *Lyrical Ballads*, he fell upon the lines

> "Knowing that Nature never did betray
> The heart that loved her."

What they meant was not clear to me [he observes], but they were a signal of the approach of something which turned out to be of the greatest importance, and altered my history.

It was a new capacity. There woke in me an aptness for the love of natural beauty, a possibility of being excited to enthusiasm by it, and of deriving a secret joy from it sufficiently strong to make me careless of the world and its pleasures. Another effect which Wordsworth had upon me, and has had on other people, was the modification, altogether unintentional on his part, of religious belief. He never dreams of attacking anybody for his creed, and yet it often becomes impossible for those who study him and care for him to be members of any orthodox religious community. . . . For some time I had no thought of heresy, but the seed was there, and was alive just as much as the seed corn is alive all the time it lies in the earth apparently dead.[21]

Commemorating the birth of his new Wordsworthian religion, Hale White in the *Autobiography* returns to the ritualistic image which earlier he had been obliged to use in the meaningless context of the old faith. "It conveyed to me no new doctrine," Mark Rutherford says of the *Lyrical Ballads*, "and yet the change it wrought in me could only be compared to that which is said to have been wrought on Paul himself by the Divine apparition."[22] Wordsworth started in him a growth which continued until gradually all his inherited beliefs, the "systems which engulfed him," fell away. This was a new birth. Hale White makes the point that the influence both of Carlyle on his father and of Wordsworth on himself was indirect, and hence pervasive: neither author directly attacks Church or creed, but the expansion of horizon that follows upon reading him makes the limitations of orthodoxy intolerable.[23] For Hale White the expansion led to a reformulation of the old doctrine in terms of the new experience; it led, that is to say, to the kind of symbolic reinterpretation which has always been forced upon those who try to reconcile new beliefs with old ones. For many in the nineteenth century this reconciliation was achieved through the "higher criticism." For Hale White it was achieved through his own creative work. It was realized by him existentially, in his fiction, as experience intensely personal. The revaluation of inherited creed became the impetus for his novel writing, a motive power that was initiated by his second, and real, "conversion" by Wordsworth. Of Wordsworth's influence he remarks in this connection that it "goes far deeper, and is far more permanent than any which is the work of Biblical critics, and it was Wordsworth and not German research which caused my expulsion from New College...."[24]

Sounding depths was dangerous in a sectarian institution. His probing into biblical problems brought Hale under suspicion. The Bible, Mark observes in the *Autobiography*, was to be the book on which their lives as ministers of the gospel were to be centered, yet no attempt was made in their curriculum actually to understand it. "I will venture to say that there was no book less understood either by students or professors. The President had a course of lectures, delivered year after year to successive generations of his pupils, upon its authenticity and inspiration. They were altogether remote from the subject...." It was Mark's

*Early Life:* The Autobiography of Mark Rutherford

own "reaching after a meaning," his refusal of classroom dogma "as communion from without and not as born from within," which constituted heresy.[25]

At this point fiction is intricately interwoven with fact in the *Autobiography*. The *Early Life* recounts Hale's expulsion from New College (now a part of the University of London and then affiliated with it), to which, at its opening in 1851, he had been transferred after three years at Cheshunt. It was with the Inaugural Lecture in fact that Hale got himself into trouble. This lecture, "The Inspiration of Scripture," delivered by the principal on the opening day, October 1, attacked the very kind of personal religious experience that Hale himself was just in the process of undergoing. (In the *Autobiography*, the Wordsworth experience occurred in Mark's third year at College.) The principal inveighed against that "self-sufficient spirit" which ignores the Bible as the source of truth and replaces it with "the religion of human nature." It was an attack on the humanism which at the time, under the influence of German thought, was leading to a more liberal interpretation of the old theology. ("It was a time in which the world outside was seething with the ferment which had been cast into it by Germany and by those in England whom Germany had influenced," but "not a fragment of it had dropped within our walls," Hale White writes of his theological school in the *Autobiography*.) In words that must have struck against the heart of the young Hale as they strike against the meaningful core of all his novels and of his matured religious outlook, the principal ridiculed "emotion, inward experience" which assumes itself to be the source of truth for giving birth to "a pious mysticism, which modifies revelation at pleasure." No wonder Hale White was to say over forty years later concerning this episode: "I can see now that if I had yielded I should have been lost forever."

On February 3 following, the senior class was examined on the contents of this lecture. Hale and two fellow students resolved to use this opportunity to give voice to some of the problems that had been troubling them. When they asked some questions about the formation of the canon and the authenticity of the separate books of the Bible, "they were immediately stopped by the Principal in summary style," and told that "this is not an open question within these walls." "How well I recollect the face of the Principal!" Hale White says. "He looked like a man who would write an invitation to tea 'within these walls.'" The three were immediately ordered to be present at a special council meeting and each one was called up separately before it and catechized, "Here," as Hale White recalls it, "are two or three of the questions, put, it will be remembered, without notice, to a youth a little over twenty, confronted by a number of solemn divines in white neckerchiefs":

"Will you explain the mode in which you conceive the sacred writers to have been influenced?"

"Do you believe a statement because it is in The Bible, or merely because it is true?"

"You are aware that there are two great parties on this question, one of which maintains that the inspiration of the Scriptures differs in kind from that of other books: The other that the difference is only one of degree. To which of these parties do you attach yourself?"

"Are you conscious of any divergence from the views expounded by the Principal in this introductory lecture?"

Their opinions were found "incompatible" with "the retention of our position as students." ("Idiomatic English," Hale White remarks, "was clearly not a strong point with the council.") On this occasion the elder White stood staunchly by his son and published his defense of freedom of thought. We know also, from the *Early Life* and from other sources, of Hale's subsequent settling in London after a year's "supplying" of a Unitarian Chapel and a fleeting, abortive attempt at teaching.[26]

## IV  Minister

At this point the *Autobiography* departs from the known facts of Hale White's life. After an account which reproduces faithfully Hale's unhappiness with his professors, omitting only the incident of his expulsion, the *Autobiography* continues with a story of Mark's life, following his four years of college, as a minister in a small town. His sense of isolation is provided with the conditions under which it can develop into its most lacerating form. The truth here projected is of a different kind from the historical. It is a poetic version of what only too easily might have been Hale's own fate, that situation of being "lost forever" which he later congratulated himself on having avoided. In the

*Early Life:* The Autobiography of Mark Rutherford

town in which Mark is incarcerated the native dullness of the inhabitants is shrouded in a ragged Puritanism which has succeeded in suffocating the sparks of human affection in almost all of them.

In his first enthusiastic sermon Mark mounts to the height of his idealism; he makes an interpretation of Christianity which is strictly personal to himself. His theme is that religions have been created to fill certain human needs. Christianity came from a poor, solitary thinker, he says; it was the religion of the unknown and the lonely. It was, in words that he does not utter, the religion of people essentially like himself, an attempt to solace the Victorian loneliness that Mark shared with the Carlyle of *Sartor Resartus*, who had said, "It was a strange isolation I then lived in. The men and women around me, even speaking with me, were but Figures. . . . In the midst of their crowded streets and assemblages, I walked solitary."[27] After the service, Mark's experience bore out the very point of his sermon. Not a soul came near him except the chapelkeeper who observed that it was raining and then went to shut up the building. Mark had to walk home in the rain with no umbrella to a cold supper by himself in a fireless room. He was overwrought and paced about for hours in hysterics. All his effort seemed the merest vanity. In the dull daylight of Monday every support had vanished, and he seemed to be sinking into a bottomless abyss. He began to develop a kind of hypochondria which was to pursue him throughout his life. Week by week a nameless horror possessed him, a sense that his mind was failing:

> For months—many months, this dreadful conviction of coming idiocy or insanity lay upon me like some poisonous reptile with its fangs driven into my very marrow, so that I could not shake it off. It went with me wherever I went, it got up with me in the morning, walked about with me all day, and lay down with me at night. I managed somehow or other to do my work, but I prayed incessantly for death; and to such a state was I reduced that I could not even make the commonest appointment for a day beforehand. The mere knowledge that something had to be done agitated me and prevented me from doing it.[28]

Then one memorable June morning during a holiday near the sea on top of one of the Devonshire hills, "I became aware of a kind of flush in the brain and a momentary relief such as I had not known since that November night. I seemed, far away on the horizon, to see just a rim of olive light low down under the edge of the leaden cloud that hung over my head, a prophecy of restoration of the sun, or at least a witness that somewhere it shone." Often, with no warning, he was to be plunged into and extricated from the Valley of the Shadow; this depression led him first to alcoholism and then to the agony of abstinence.

Such is Mark's introduction to his vocation of Calvinist minister. Mark is undergoing here the trial by dullness and isolation which is to be the lot of all Hale White's heroes. He prefigures their central religious quest, whether it be in terms of the old Calvinistic faith with its image of a Christ lonely like themselves and kin to them, or in terms of a newer humanism with its image of a friend. The theme is always to be the meaning of religion as relatedness, cosmic and human, in a world inhabited by the lonely crowd.

## V  *Freethinkers*

In the *Autobiography*, therefore, the characters representing the old orthodoxy become the villains, cold and petty; while the freethinkers are the vital, companionable people, closest to the original Christian ideal. This ironic contrast is to appear again in the later stories. Even as for John Wesley, Newman, and Arnold, the central evil for Hale White was not disbelief but "nominal" belief.[29] In the *Autobiography*, as an example of nominal orthodoxy, is Mr. Snale, deacon and draper, exceedingly "genteel," with "the marked peculiarity that he hardly ever said anything, no matter how disagreeable it might be, without stretching as if in a smile his thin little lips," and with a way of talking about the "leedies" "more odious than the way of a debauchee."[30]

Characteristically, it is on an issue of public welfare, one outside the bounds of his rigid concept of religion, that Snale clashes with Mark. The town's water supply is polluted by sewage. Mark has supported a movement to improve it. Snale writes an anonymous letter to the paper expressing shock that a minister of the gospel should meddle in politics. The old militant faith of Cromwell's army has in the person of Snale degenerated into a monstrous formalism, stripped of its relation to actual living. Contrasted to Snale's perfidy is the integrity of Edward Gibbon

*Early Life:* The Autobiography of Mark Rutherford

Mardon, the town's professional freethinker, a type of the Age of Reason, as his middle name intimates. In Mardon, Mark finds the companion he has long sought, a man in his own way somewhat like the "poor, solitary thinker" Mark had represented Christ to be in his first sermon.

Mardon is intellectually, however, very much a Victorian, representing the skeptical "scientific" strain which descended from eighteenth-century rationalism. What binds Mark to him is his honesty and curiosity, the essential *seriousness* which was Hale White's first requirement in a friend. Mardon combines atheism with the moral strength Hale White respected in such truly religious men as Caleb Morris and his own father. Intellectually, Mardon battles with Mark, putting the young man's dogma to the test of skepticism. Through Mardon, Mark comes into contact with forces of which his carefully hedged childhood has been innocent. He is disturbed and jarred as he has not been jolted by the more expansive influence of Wordsworth. For the first time his basic assumption has been questioned—the existence of God. The living friend, Mardon, whom he has gained, costs Mark the loss of his imaginary one, Jesus: "The dissolution of Jesus into mythologic vapour was nothing less than the death of a friend dearer to me then than any other friend whom I knew." With pitiless logic Mardon also erodes Mark's faith in a life beyond the grave. Another trial begins for Mark, the soul crisis which again and again grew out of the conflicting currents of nineteenth-century thought: "Mardon's talk darkened my days and nights."[31] In this brief statement lies concentrated the bewilderment and pessimism of the age.

Mardon has a daughter, Mary, one of those creatures from a foreign clime—intellectual and moral—who, appearing suddenly on the scene, vanquish Hale White's Puritan heroes. Mary has her father's candor, simplicity, and quiet strength. Mark's attraction to her is instant. Small, exquisitely graceful, she is even physically unlike the daughters of Dissent that Mark has known (to one of whom he is even at the moment engaged). It is as though for Hale White the Puritan atmosphere robbed the women of their vitality, as though a largess of free thought were the condition of feminine attractiveness. Like Pauline Caillaud—daughter of a professed atheist and revolutionary in the *Revolution in Tanner's Lane,* the beloved of its hero, who is fleeing from a sharp, Puritan wife—these exotic women are to the English women like "a wild sea gull in a farm yard of peaceful, clucking, brown-speckled fowl." Unhappily, union with the exciting stranger in all the novels is frustrated by either sudden death or rejection. In the *Autobiography* this pattern is set. Mark breaks a long, protracted engagement to Ellen, daughter of a deacon and a fellow teacher at Sunday school back home (of Ellen we know nothing significant beside this), just at the point where the girl expects him at last to marry her. "I saw before me the long days of wedded life with no sympathy, and I shuddered when I thought of what I should do with such a wife."[32]

### VI  *John Chapman and George Eliot*

Mark's moorings have in many ways been loosened. He has become a stranger in his world. His story is in this respect like a case history of Victorian bewilderment, of that sense of the loss of an intelligible universe which has reappeared in our time and been called the sense of the "absurd."[33] Under the assaults of Mardon's skepticism, his faith totters. This struggle reduces him to such a condition of doubt that he feels finally obliged to resign his ministry. In a scene resilient with irony he parts from orthodoxy as represented in the person of Mr. Snale. The next step is Unitarianism. Following the path of least resistance, he accepts a living in a neighboring town where "a few descendants of the eighteenth-century heretics still testify against three Gods in one and the deity of Jesus Christ."[34] But the "heresy" of Unitarianism is dead to him; he has passed beyond that stage. And the emotional response is just as dead here as among the Independents. He finds the same absence of personal affection, the same suffering. One day he meets a butterfly collector, who points the moral of stoical resignation which is to become the theme of Hale White's next novel, *Mark Rutherford's Deliverance*. The butterfly collector has been saved from the brutishness of life by a scientifically significant pursuit, one that transcends personal problems. Astronomy was to become for Hale White himself, and for the heroine of *Miriam's Schooling*, such a therapy.

From this point on the *Autobiography* again corresponds fairly closely to what we know of the actual facts of Hale White's own

*Early Life:* The Autobiography of Mark Rutherford

life. The prelude to Mark's "emancipation" is a two-day attempt at school mastering, an experience to which in his *Early Life* Hale White traces the origin of the melancholia that pursued him through the years.[35] In the *Autobiography* he amplifies the traumatic scene. After the cold supper in an empty school room at Stoke Newington, gazing out at the empty distances to London illuminated in the night "like some unnatural dawn," he is "overcome with the most dreadful sense of loneliness. . . . Reflecting on what I suffered then, I cannot find any solid ground for it, and yet there are not half-a-dozen days or nights of my life which remain with me like that one. I was beside myself with a kind of terror, which I cannot further explain. . . . It is many years ago since that evening but while I write I am at the window still, and the yellow flare of the city is still in my eyes." The next day Mark finds a substitute for his job and flees into the heart of London. He finds work with a publisher, Wollaston, who we know was John Chapman, publisher of the *Westminster Review*, the liberal medium of such "utilitarians" as John Stuart Mill. Founded by Bentham, it was dedicated to "French principles" and science. Chapman himself was a militant non-believer who had published such books as the English version of Strauss's *Leben Jesu*. Before hiring Hale, Chapman asked him one test question: Did he believe in miracles? Caught between two dogmatisms, Hale said his answer must be both "yes" and "no"—for while he disbelieved in the fact of certain miracles, he believed in the spiritual truth set forth in them. In this answer Hale expressed that poetic reinterpretation of the old creed which was to become the key to his fiction. The answer was allowed to pass. "As the New College tested my orthodoxy," Hale White remarks, "so Chapman tested my heresy."

For all his emancipation, however, Wollaston (Chapman) is shown to be essentially shallow. His atheism is of the same "nominal" kind as was Snale's orthodoxy. His is the "heartless emptiness" that Hale White contemns whether it parades under the guise of religious piety or of free thought. Wollaston had, as Mark puts it, picked up a few phrases; but his ideas, never having been cultivated, bore no fruit. They were "like hard stones which he rattled in his pocket." In this respect Wollaston, like Snale, is contrasted to Mardon, whose convictions were held in depth. "A mental comparison of the two," says Mark of Mardon and Wollaston, "often told me what I had been told over and over again, that what we believe is not of so much importance as the path by which we travel to it." In a letter to his father, written in 1853, Hale's second year in London with Chapman, he makes a similar observation about Chapman. "With all that you say I most cordially agree. Most especially with what you say about cold negativism. Mr. Chapman is nothing so much of a negation merely as many of his books are but I see and must see infinitely more of this heartless emptiness both in books and men than I ever saw before, and this drives me back again to all my old eternal friends who appear more than ever perfect, and Jesus above them all."[36]

The highlight of Hale White's early years in London was his friendship with George Eliot, assistant editor of the *Westminster Review* and fellow lodger in the Chapman household. She was then (1852-1854) a comparatively unknown young writer, but her distinction as a human being was to Hale White immediately discernible. He has given us a glimpse of her in a letter to the *Athenaeum*: "She occupied two dark but very quiet rooms. . . . She was then not quite what she appeared to be in later years. She never reserved herself, but always said what was best in her at the moment, even when no special demand was made upon her. Consequently she found out what was best in everybody. I have not heard better talk than hers, even when there was nobody to listen but myself and the ordinary members of the Chapman household."[37] In the *Autobiography* she appears as Theresa, niece of Wollaston, the publisher. Mark is struck by her incisive thinking, her vigorous, firm gait, her way of looking straight at the person with whom she is speaking. He is struck also by her beautiful hair, yellowish and naturally waved, and by her grayish blue eyes, "generally soft and tender, but convertible into the keenest flash," as he records of her in his notebook.[38] But above all he is struck by her talk, which, again in his notebook, Hale White precisely delineates: "The style of Miss Evans's conversation was perfect; it was quite natural, but never slip-shod, and the force and sharpness of her thought were never lost in worn phrases." To Mark in the *Autobiography* she is a constant study, unclassified as a human being and certainly as a woman by any standards he has ever known. At first he thinks her hard, but then he finds by accident that nearly all her earn-

*Early Life:* The Autobiography of Mark Rutherford

ings are given to support a couple of poor relations (a point Hale White also makes in his essay on George Eliot in his published journal). She delights in music (George Eliot introduced Hale White to Glück's *Orfeo* and played Beethoven for him).

To Mark, Miss Evans gives what all his life he has been seeking—intelligent companionship. The portrait of her in the *Autobiography* resembles somewhat that of Mary Mardon in her directness and her touch of unconventionality. Even more, it resembles that of the finely tempered, clear-headed type of woman that Hale White is to honor in his later novels, notably in *Clara Hopgood*. "At times she appeared passionless," he says of Theresa, "so completely did her intellect dominate, and so superior was she to all the little arts and weaknesses of women; but this was a criticism she contradicted continually."[39] On one occasion a stupid blunder at his job caused all Mark's pent up feeling of worthlessness in a life of repeated failures to well up: "I was beside myself, and I threw myself on my knees, burying my face in Theresa's lap and sobbing convulsively. She did not repel me, but she gently passed her fingers through my hair. Oh the transport of that touch! It was as if water had been poured on a burnt hand, or some miraculous Messiah had soothed the delirium of a fever-stricken sufferer, and replaced his visions of torment with dreams of Paradise. She gently lifted me up and as I rose I saw her eyes too were wet."[40] After that he "worshipped Theresa, and was overcome with unhesitating absorbing love for her." Hale White was to remark later of George Eliot, "I could worship that woman."[41] George Eliot-Theresa, like Dorothy Wordsworth, possessed for him that rare combination of qualities with which he endowed the heroines of his novels: intellectual force, feminine softness, and unconventional, because forthright, behavior.

The *Autobiography* ends on the note of Mardon's death, softened, as Mark's earlier suffering has been, by the balm of nature's beauty. Mark sits with Mary through the night at the deathbed of his friend, and in the morning a magnificent sunrise appears over perfectly smooth water. "Death was in the chamber, but the surpassing splendour of the pageant outside arrested us, and we sat awed and silent."[42] The note of the next novel, *The Deliverance* is here again struck, and it continues through a little epilogue by the make-believe "editor" Reuben Shapcott on the later course of Mark's life. Mary died of a cold caught at her father's funeral. A crisis in Mark's life seemed to take a turn just then; "he became less involved in his old speculations, and more devoted to other pursuits." Symbolically, the butterfly catcher, who earlier had trained Mark's thoughts toward stoical resignation, reappeared to lead him back to the green lanes of Surrey on butterfly hunts. Eventually, "Reuben Shapcott" tells us, Mark got employment with a newspaper, and, like Hale White himself, a seat in the press gallery of the House of Commons. Shapcott concludes: "A more perfect friend I never knew. . . ."

Here, then, is a record of a man's effort to find himself in that Victorian scene which Arnold figured as a darkling plain where ignorant armies clash by night. What strikes us, because we know Hale White to have been one of the most secretive of men, is its unaffected self-revelation. This self grows as it is stimulated by the forces of the age. "It may be doubted," says one historian of the English novel, "if any writer has ever rendered mental agony with such power as Mark Rutherford. Doubt is for him not a philosphical balancing of probabilities; it is a cruel force rending him in twain."[43]

## VII  *"Plain-glass" Style*

The *Autobiography*, in some ways the best book Hale White ever wrote, is also his first. It was written in haste during hours snatched from an inordinately busy life. Mrs. White tells us that "he remembers writing the first book, The Autobiography, at 'extraordinary high-pressure.' He was then at work every night at the House of Commons, and he wrote in the mornings, 4:30."[44] Yet his style is such as would suggest leisurely days of careful writing. It is, in fact, the expression of his character. It bears witness to the rigorous purity of the tradition in which he had been reared. He aimed not properly at "style" but at directness, as did the best Puritan authors, men like Baxter, Bunyan, and Defoe.

This tradition was transmitted to Hale White from the start through his own father, of whom he said: "There was one endowment for which he was remarkable, the purity of the English he spoke and wrote."[45] The elder White consciously modeled himself on William Cobbett, but the seventeenth-century Puritan preachers, in whom he was deeply read, had their influence too. William White, Sr., once quoted from one of those old divines, William Burkitt, a sentence which serves as a touchstone for Hale White's own literary taste: "Painted glass is very beautiful, but plain glass is the most useful and lets in the most light."[46] Hale White's was always to be a "plain-glass" style. He was revolted by vulgar show of any kind. Thus he praises Mary, Mardon's daughter: "I noticed one peculiarity about her manner of talking, and that was perfect simplicity. There was no sort of effort or strain in anything she said, no attempt by emphasis of words to make up for weakness of thought, and no compliance with that vulgar and most disagreeable habit of using intense language to describe what is not intense in itself."[47] This last phrase might almost be taken as Hale White's injunction for writing, as well as for speaking. Lady Robert Cecil remarks from her personal knowledge of Hale White that "his talk was very like his writing, and both were, I suppose, a singularly exact expression of his thought."[48]

Together with his fine restraint, Hale White has a peculiarly gentle kind of wit, which is never allowed to become too obvious or to cut too deeply. It shows itself typically in a sober irony, which may escape all but the alert. One laughs, Sperry has said, "not with Gargantuan laughter which spends itself in one outbreak, but rather with the quiet smile of the 'Comic Muse, grave and sisterly' who, looking upon this world, compresses her lips."[49] Hale White could thus touch lightly on the "economy" of those good Unitarians who offered him "potatoes *or* cabbage" at dinner, or the flexible orthodoxy of the respectable Anglican parishioners who, "notwithstanding the denunciations of the parson, preferred tea with some taste in it from a Unitarian to the insipid wood-flavoured stuff which was sold by the grocer who believed in the Trinity."[50]

CHAPTER 3

# *Later Life:*
# Mark Rutherford's Deliverance

THE *Deliverance* is about Mark's life in London and the ways he found to escape from himself. Biographically, this was the most vigorous period in Hale White's own life, from his early twenties (he got his first London job in 1854, at the age of twenty-two), into his fifties; yet of these years the essential information is meager, though the external facts are multitudinous enough. For the essential life of the Hale White we know is an inner one, assiduously concealed from his colleagues at Whitehall and from the world at large. The dream-like years of his childhood and the *sturm und drang* of his young manhood he has recorded in detail. The astonishingly productive evening of his life is amply documented in letters, notebooks, and a diary. Yet for the days of his prime, the only significant record is this *Deliverance;* and it is presented under a heavy veil of fiction.

For the fiction deviates considerably from fact. We may surmise that of these years, when he was busily occupied making his way in life, there is less to tell. His exuberant sensibility, under attack from extraordinary pressures of work and anxiety, was kept from extinction only by the heroic expedient of getting up at about four every morning for a few quiet hours of reading and writing. Catherine Macdonald Maclean has in her biography of Hale White carefully chronicled the events of this period: his domestic cares with six children (two of whom died early) and an incurably ill wife;[1] his career in the civil service (first for four years, 1854-1858, in the Registrar-General's Office, where he scrutinized monotonously "all the livelong day" entries of births, deaths, and marriages; then for thirty-four years, 1858-1892, in the Admiralty, where he rose to a position of responsibility as Assistant-Director in the Purchase Department for the

*Later Life:* Mark Rutherford's *Deliverance*

British Navy); and his extra work as London correspondent for a number of newspapers like the *Aberdeen Herald*, writing a weekly column of "political education" based on his regular attendance at the House of Commons.

Life for Hale White was a grinding day-to-day existence: after his regular office work, going to the House, coming home at six or seven; writing up his articles after dinner, often till quite late; and getting up before dawn the next morning. He was constantly plagued by the anxiety that he would not finish his office duties at the Admiralty in time and so would miss promotion. Yet during these years—in the last dozen or so before his retirement in 1883—all but the last of his novels were written; and his great translation from the Latin of Spinoza's *Ethic*, made some twenty years before, was reworked and published with a long introductory essay (1883). In the light of such a life, there is more of a need in the *Deliverance* to feign, to disguise the literal truth, here so much further removed than was the story of the *Autobiography* from that poetic truth which it is Mark Rutherford's function to embody as the *alter ego* of his author.

In the *Autobiography* Mark appeared shaken by the melee which disturbed his time and which shattered not a few in the conflict between belief and doubt. He had been a minister without a gospel, finely attuned to the pervasive air of gloom. Now in the *Deliverance* we find the struggle less severe, but not because he has reconciled the issues. The issues themselves have become less urgent. Hale White prefaces the novel with a motto from *Macbeth*: "Come what come may,/Time and the hour run through the roughest day." Bunyan had written, in the vein Hale White was here tracing out and in words which probably suggested to him the title for his book: "As to thy burden be content to bear it, until thou comest to the place of deliverance; for there it will fall from thy back of itself."

Of the two kinds of heroes possible, the enduring one like Job and the rebellious one like Prometheus, Hale White's early protagonists (the men—Mark Rutherford and Zachariah Coleman) are of the former type, heroic in their stamina. But his later protagonists (the women—Miriam, Catharine Furze, Clara and Madge Hopgood) are of the latter kind. It is as though endurance were for Hale White the stronger, more masculine virtue. No other novelist, in fact, is like him in his subtle and honest evocation of suffering as a source of strength. Appropriately enough, his powerful analysis of the Book of Job is usually included under the same cover with the *Deliverance*.

## I  *The Stoic*

The *Deliverance* is the story of a man older, more subdued than the Mark of the *Autobiography*, one for whom the edge of youthful pain has been blunted. And deliverance is found, not salvation. It is a *modus vivendi*, a happiness only in the stoical sense of absence from pain. It is, in short, deliverance from evil. Matthew Arnold struck the true note of Hale White's attitude in his poetry. "Empedocles on Etna," as Arnold describes it in his Preface to his Poems of 1853, develops a situation whereby "a continuous state of mental distress is prolonged, unrelieved by incident, hope or resistance; in which there is everything to be endured, nothing to be done." Hale White's heroes are heroic, not in their deeds but in their endurance. The stoical attitude, disciplined and deliberate, was peculiarly adapted to the Victorian temper. Arnold devoted one of his *Essays in Criticism* (1865) to the emperor-stoic, Marcus Aurelius, and another to the not dissimilar thought of Spinoza, Hale White's special favorite.

Hale White's own concern with the stoical view during these years when his early novels were being written is suggested by an essay he published in 1880 on "Marcus Antoninus." In it he adumbrates the theme of the *Deliverance*, published five years later: "Antoninus was engaged in a continuous wrestle to provide himself with thoughts which would overcome in the battle with life and death—thoughts which would make his existence tolerable and prevent anxiety about its termination." Antoninus' reconciliation is not an intellectual one between belief and doubt but a moral one between himself and nature. His consolation, says Hale White, may seem "meager" compared with "the magnificent promises of the religious," but it is "based upon the everlasting adamant" and is not to be shaken by any "Higher Criticism." The works of Antoninus and of Epictetus are "the most nearly complete series of solutions which the world possesses of its most pressing problems." He concludes his essay with words that read like a prophecy of the careers of his two principal heroes, Mark Rutherford and Zachariah Coleman:

## *Later Life:* Mark Rutherford's *Deliverance*

There is assuredly no spectacle in the world of diviner interest to us than that of the hero who labours perpetually to fashion for himself a creed upon which he may lean, who does not content himself with shirking the duty imposed upon him, or with drugging himself into forgetfulness of it, but faces it. The blood is poured forth in secret, and there is no prospect of public triumph or applause. . . . Heroism! Who that has been called upon to undertake this task, who that has had to fight this fight, will not say that even the Persians in the pass of Thermopylae exacted from the Lacedemonians an endurance and a courage less exalted.[2]

The fresh secular breezes stirring across the nineteenth century have in the *Deliverance* ventilated the stale chapel air that had suffocated the young Mark of the *Autobiography*. Wordsworth, Spinoza, Carlyle, and the Stoics opened his understanding to the "everlasting adamant" of natural law. Mark is no longer possessed by those "magnificent promises of the religious," the mirage of a universe of love, which led to his grappling with a brutish reality (what Samuel Beckett calls "the mess") and to his consequent frustration and despair. He can, as a result, "be satisfied with the limitations of his own nature" (a phrase from an essay called "Principles," which was published under the same cover with the *Deliverance*).[3] This lesson was the one the butterfly catcher in the *Autobiography* had tried to convey to a younger Mark.[4] In a scene which recalls Carlyle's *Sartor Resartus*—Professor Teufelsdröckh's embrace of The Everlasting Yea after he has realized that "It is only with Renunciation . . . that Life, properly speaking, can be said to begin" and after he has asked himself "What Act of Legislature was there that *thou* shouldst be Happy?"—Mark is shown as casting off the bondage of his discontent:

I remember the day and the very spot on which it flashed into me, like a sudden burst of the sun's rays, that I had no right to this or that—to so much happiness, or even so much virtue. What title-deeds could I show for such a right? Straightway it seemed as if the centre of a whole system of dissatisfaction were removed, and as if the system collapsed. God, creating from his infinite resources a whole infinitude of beings, had created me with a definite position on the scale, and that position only could I claim. Cease the trick of contrast. If I can by any means get myself to consider myself alone without reference to others, discontent will vanish.[5]

## II  *Christian Socialism*

Mark's work was to report speeches at the House of Commons, a position he secured through a "relative" who "held some office" there. This is an instance of Hale White's fidelity to fact which inclines us in general to trust his account in the *Deliverance*. We know that Hale's father, doorkeeper of the House, facilitated his admission to the gallery; here he took notes for his London Letters to various newspapers.[6] "These letters were a great trouble to me," Mark says. "I was always conscious of writing so much of which I was not certain, and so much which was indifferent to me. The unfairness of parties haunted me. But I continued to write because I saw no other way of getting a living." Not above once or twice, in the more than a thousand columns that Hale White wrote between 1861 and 1883, did his labors, if we can trust the words of Mark Rutherford, meet with the slightest public recognition.

Nevertheless, Mark's old interests still persisted, though in another form. He found himself in league with an idealistic friend, M'Kay, in a project which involved the regeneration of London's submerged tenth by means of a new vital religious force, "by inspiration spreading itself suddenly." The odds against them, the mid-Victorian slums, were overwhelming: "the sky over their heads is mud, the earth is mud under their feet, the muddy houses stretch in long rows, black, gaunt and uniform." The lives of these people were brutish and monotonous to desperation. Regeneration was impossible, the two friends soon found out. Neither the teaching of Christ nor any known stimulus could counterbalance London's back streets.[7]

It is this active engagement with life that saves Mark. While in the *Autobiography* Mark had found a friend, Mardon, who tore away his connection with his past, in the *Deliverance* he finds one in M'Kay who helps him establish ties with a new world. Both friends have aided him in his religious quest—the first in clearing the ground of irrelevant dogma; the second, in opening up for him the possibilities of a workable religion. "He was firmly persuaded," says Mark of M'Kay, "that we need religion, poor and rich alike. We need some controlling influence to bind together our scattered energies."[8] This was the kind of social gospel, of a personal and applied Christianity, which the

*Later Life:* Mark Rutherford's *Deliverance*

younger Mark had in the *Autobiography* himself anticipated in his first sermon and upon which Hale White's next novel, *The Revolution in Tanner's Lane*, focuses. M'Kay gets Mark to rent a room with him in Drury Lane, his object being to keep it open "as a place to which those who wished might resort at different times, and find some quietude, instruction, and what fortifying thoughts he could collect to enable men to endure their almost unendurable sufferings."[9] Hale White in his early London days, in 1859, had similarly rented a room for the purpose of providing just such human fellowship in the heart of industrial London, a place of public communion which all men, especially the unorthodox, could join.[10]

This project of Hale White, like that of Mark in the *Deliverance*, bears the imprint of the religious–political movement known as Christian Socialism, which in 1848 was started by Frederick Denison Maurice and Charles Kingsley. Their purpose was to rescue socialism from its ill repute and to show that properly understood it meant simply the application of Christian principles to industrial organization. They started a weekly paper, *Politics for the People*, which in its first leading article stated the theme that Hale White developed in the *Deliverance*: "Politics have too long been separated from Christianity. . . ."[11] To this idea Kingsley himself devoted *Alton Locke* (1850). There the hero is befriended by a Chartist called Sandy Mackaye, whose name, spelled differently, is the same as that of the M'Kay who befriended Mark.[12] The Drury Lane project of Mark and M'Kay exhibits, in general, the social awareness that followed on the secularization of religion in the Victorian period, that fusing of the generically Christian and the specifically humanitarian which became the theme of, for example, the Salvation Army, founded (with military trimmings) by William Booth in 1865. The Christian Socialists themselves established a project which may well have been in Hale White's mind when he wrote of Drury Lane. This project was a Workingman's College in Great Ormond Street, where Ruskin directed the art classes and wrote for the cause, applying his own Evangelical conscience to the humanitarian socialism which occupied his later years. This Christian, Evangelical background, so evident in Ruskin's own social gospel,[13] was determinative in the development of modern British socialism and the concept of the Welfare State toward which the *Deliverance* is groping. Contrary to the Marxian socialists (largely Continental), who considered Christianity "an immoral illusion," the English Socialists from Kingsley to the Fabians accepted Christianity as their natural ally. It is to this development that the *Deliverance* essentially belongs.

Both Maurice and Kingsley were in Hale White's own mind associated with that expansion of his own religious outlook which was signalized by his expulsion from New College. It is their letters congratulating the elder White on his defense of his son that Hale White reproduces in his *Early Life*. Kingsley's letter dwelt on the decline of orthodoxy. "This is only one symptom," Kingsley said of the Whites' disaffection, "of a great and growing movement, which must end in the absolute destruction of 'Orthodox dissent' among the educated classes . . . if your son would like to write me about these matters, I do believe before God who sees me write, that as one who has been through what he has, and more, I may have something to tell him, or at least to set him thinking over."[14]

### III  *Drury Lane Theology*

Scorn for established religion and bitterness at the social evils to which it remains oblivious are in the *Deliverance* reminiscent of Blake. (In *The Norfolk News* of January 15, 1876, Hale White tells of a dispute among members of a London High Church congregation over whether or not some "dirty children" were to be allowed to attend services, some of the members objecting on the grounds that "the children stank and had fleas." The churchwardens, he reports, declared in favor of "the salvation of the clean.")[15] With a Naturalism quite as trenchant as Zola's own or as that of George Gissing later on in the century, he revives the slums of Victorian London in such passages as the following:

As we walked over the Drury Lane gratings of the cellars a most foul stench came up, and one in particular I remember to this day. A man half dressed pushed open a broken window beneath us, just as we passed by, and there issued such a blast of corruption, made up of gases bred by filth, air breathed and rebreathed a hundred times, charged with odours of unnameable personal uncleanliness and disease, that I staggered to the gutter with a qualm I could scarcely conquer. At the doors of the houses stood grimy women with their

## Later Life: Mark Rutherford's Deliverance

arms folded and their hair disordered. Grimier boys and girls had tied a rope to broken railings, and were swinging on it. The common door to a score of lodgings stood ever open, and the children swarmed up and down the stairs carrying with them patches of mud every time they came in from the street. . . . The shops were open [it is Sunday] most of them exhibiting a most miscellaneous collection of goods, such as bacon cut in slices, fire-wood, a few loaves of bread, and sweetmeats in dirty bottles. Fowls, strange to say, black as the flagstones, walked in and out of these shops, or descended into the dark areas.[16]

The cities of the world, Mark began to understand, were largely jungles impaled below a filthy gloom of sky in which the poor were herded. He had not realized until he came into actual contact with them "how far away the classes which lie at the bottom of great cities are from those above them; how completely they are inaccessible to motives which act upon ordinary human beings, and how deeply they are sunk beyond ray of sun or stars, immersed in the selfishness naturally begotten of their incessant struggle for existence and the incessant warfare with society. . . . Our civilization seemed nothing but a thin film or crust lying over a volcanic pit, and I often wondered whether some day the pit would not break up through it and destroy us all."[17]

Mark got to know two or three of the slum dwellers who came regularly to their little room. Their stories read like illustrations of an inferno just beyond Mark's own threshold. One of them is indeed a sad caricature of Mark, a Calvinist without a faith, plagued by metaphysical doubts, and for his livelihood copying addresses all day long with a monotony that daily stuns him—a job that recalls the monotonous copying that was Hale White's own work for five years in the Registrar-General's Office. The message which Mark and M'Kay have to offer these desperate people is that of the "deliverance" itself: to find contentment with one's lot in life. This is their "Drury Lane theology"; it recalls only too forcibly the harsh definition of religion as the opium of the people.

This social work is as much a therapy for Mark as it is for his "cases." He is ready now to practice for himself the theology of Drury Lane. The crucial proving and implementing of this new attitude appears in his relations with Ellen, the girl whom, at the time he fell in love with the exotic and unattainable Mary Mardon, in the *Autobiography*, he had rejected. The Ellen he finds again has also been matured by adversity—marriage to a brutal husband. She has been supported in her suffering by the old faith, which even thus demonstrates its peculiar strength to Mark, who had rejected it together with the girl. In essence, the virtue of the old religion, divested of its metaphysical aspect, is that of Mark's own Drury Lane nonbeliever's gospel. It is the moral virtue of submission to circumstance which is the theme of the *Deliverance*.

Untroubled by the compulsive speculativeness of a Mark, Ellen is still Hale White's Englishwoman, drawing sustenance from the conventions Hale White earlier satirized, but which he now revaluates in a kindlier light. For Mark, this is a reconstruction. His is no longer a youthful ardor, as for Mary Mardon, but a flame that has to be carefully tended. "My love for Ellen was great," he says, "but I discovered that even such love as this could not be left to itself. It wanted perpetual cherishing. The lamp, if it was to burn brightly, required daily trimming, for people become estranged and indifferent, not so much by open quarrel or serious difference, as by the intervention of trifles which need but the smallest, although continuous effort for their removal. . . . If through relapse into idleness we do not attempt to bring soul and heart into active communion day by day, what wonder if this once exalted relationship become vulgar and mean?"[18]

Hale White's partiality for the unconventional, un-English type of woman is, however, not absent in this novel. It emerges in a long digression on the history of Ellen's unhappy marriage before her return, beginning with the story of "Miss Leroy," the mother of Ellen's husband. Like the Theresa (George Eliot) of the *Autobiography*, Miss Leroy is unclassifiable in the early Victorian scene, a prefigurement of the "new woman" of the later part of the century. She shocked her neighbors by walking out alone on starry nights or by going at four o'clock on summer mornings to a neighboring village church to read *De Imitatione Christi* on its porch. She told a man once, "to his face," that if she loved him and he loved her, they could, for aught she cared, just sign each other's forehead with a cross and let that represent their marriage ceremony. This remark quite upset his mother, Mark adds; "she repeated it now and then for fifty years."

In contrast to the good English housewives, whose conscien-

*Later Life:* Mark Rutherford's Deliverance

tious tidiness Hale White associated with a cold and niggardly nature, Miss Leroy "cared nothing for the linen-closet, the spotless bed hangings, and the bright poker which were the true household gods of the respectable women of those days."[19] It was furthermore believed by Miss Leroy's neighbors that she bathed daily, a habit they considered "weakening" and "somehow connected with ethical impropriety." In all her behavior, "She was a person whom nobody could have created in writing a novel, she was so inconsistent." Her home like herself was warm and permissive, a haven from Puritan rigidity. Hers were the wild garden and the straggling orchard that made up the paradise of Mark's childhood. She was one of the very, very few, Mark recalls, "who knew how to love a child." With a touch of the alien and exotic in her French name and nature, Miss Leroy lived among the English "as an Arabian bird . . . in one of our barnyards with the ordinary barnyard fowls."[20]

How far Mark has descended from his ideal in marrying Ellen may now be gauged. This is but another example of his "deliverance," his acquiescence to circumstance. It is not Ellen who in this descent is being judged, but Mark. Ellen is still very much of a blank to us, in spite of the long digression on her life, which is devoted mostly to other people with whom she is connected. It is as though Hale White is unable to present dramatically the solid English virtues he wants us to acknowledge in Ellen. She fulfills her function in giving Mark the support he has always needed. He is now able to shield himself against the outrages of fortune. The parallel to Hale White's own life, which has appeared implicit in Mark's relationship with his wife, becomes explicit when Mark takes on an office job to supplement his income from the newspaper work.

We are here introduced to the world of clerks that Hale White got to know so well and we gain a sharper sense of his alienation within it, opposed as it was to all he lived for. "I never liked it," he curtly said of it.[21] Mark is shocked by the obscenity of his city-bred colleagues. They in turn twit him. But his continued silence eventually wins him immunity. ("He told me that when he was a young man, at the office," Mrs. White records, "he had to endure plenty of . . . ribald talk, but he never joined in it, and never laughed at it. . . . 'Oh, of course I got called names—Pious, I think was the word.'")[22] Mark's "stratagem of defense" is never to betray to a soul at the office anything about himself, even as Hale White made himself as anonymous as possible, concealing his true nature under the mask of a stern disciplinarian. "Nobody knew anything about me," Mark says, "whether I was married or single, where I lived or what I thought upon a single subject of importance. I cut off my office life from my life at home so completely that I was two selves, and my true self was not stained by contact with my other self."[23]

This preservation of the true self, as far as it applies to Hale White, is of great interest in the light of his later development. The ways of living during this period hold much of the clue to the unique spectacle of his later life—that of a civil servant who not only wrote novels, but ones with the tact and vigor of a carefully cultivated, leisurely mind. We know how Hale White snatched his leisure from pre-dawn hours. The *Deliverance* suggests something of the origin of this need: "I began to calculate that my life consisted of nothing but the brief spaces allowed to me for rest, and these brief spaces I could not enjoy because of their brevity. There was some excuse for me. Never could there be any duty incumbent upon man much more inhuman and devoid of interest than my own. How often I thought about my friend Clark [the Drury Lane clerk who copied addresses all day long], and his experiences became mine. The whole day I did nothing but write, and what I wrote called forth no single faculty of mind. Nobody who has not tried such an occupation can possibly forecast the strange habits, humours, fancies, and diseases which after a time it breeds."[24] Obscenity was the outlet the other clerks used. One of Hale White's main themes is the degenerative influence of routine.

## IV  Routine

Routine is the brutalization of the human spirit against which he, like Carlyle and Ruskin and Dickens, inveighs—men losing their dignity in country torpor or in city drudgery; women, their gentleness in the petty strivings of "respectability." It is this which rots in the core of the unhappy marriages he is ever depicting—one partner, sunk in brutish routine; the other, isolated in a world of ideas. Hale White's novels are as much a testament to the cultivated spirit as are the essays of Matthew Arnold. Hale White's faith in this spirit is his most valuable inheritance

*Later Life:* Mark Rutherford's Deliverance

from his background of Dissent, a tradition of aristocratic lineage, reaching back to such founders as Bunyan and Milton. However, the preservation of this inheritance through thirty-eight years of duty essentially "inhuman and devoid of interest" and its prompt fulfillment upon the first opportunity are a tribute to the strength and viability of the man himself. He reveals the immediate origin of this strength, almost inadvertently, when in the *Autobiography* he shows the kind of influence Wordsworth had on the young Mark: "Of more importance, too, than the decay of systems was the birth of a habit of inner reference and a dislike to occupy myself with anything which did not in some way or other touch the soul, or was not the illustration or embodiment of some spiritual law."[25]

Such "inner reference" is the vibrant core of the Protestant, and particularly the nonconformist, attitude. Wittingly or not, Mark's development toward the freer reaches of Wordsworth had been prepared for by the values and emphases of his old religion, and these remained his succor through the years of alienation recounted in the *Deliverance*. In revolt against his office work "there was developed an appetite which was voracious for all that was best."[26] Mark's evenings were devoted to this. Speculation, however, had deeply seared him; it found no place in this new life. "Philosophy and religion," he says, "I did not touch."[27]

V *"An Old Official Mill-Horse"*

Even these arduous years were not without an occasional respite, when a man could indulge that love for nature bred into him during his earliest days—"in the solitary meadows and in the water." In the close of the *Autobiography*, and in that of the *Deliverance*, the dominant note is on the elevating and joy-giving power of nature. London with its cloud of smoke is left behind: "We sat down on a floor made of the leaves of last year. At midday the stillness was profound, broken only by the softest of whispers descending from the great trees which spread over us their protecting arms. Every now and then it died down almost to nothing, and then slowly swelled and died again, as if the gods of the place were engaged in divine and harmonious talk . . . summer dying in such fashion filled our hearts with repose, and even more than repose—with actual joy."[28]

Hale White goes through with his little game of deception,

and now under the guise of Reuben Shapcott appends a note to the effect that "a year after this last holiday my friend was dead and buried." As a matter of fact, we know that after the task of breadwinning was over, the precise opposite happened: an astounding birth of interest and activity occurred, which testifies to the energy the man must have had. Not only fiction, but philosophy and literary criticism occupied him until the very end of his eighty-one years. He himself modestly explains about this round of work to a friend: "You see I am an old official mill-horse, and was obliged when real work ceased to go round and round just for nothing but because I had always been used to that kind of motion."[29]

Though the literal truth is modified, the essential truth of Hale White's life shines through the *Deliverance* as it did through the *Autobiography*. The *Autobiography* gives us the story of disillusionment on the part of a young idealist who sought the City of God in mid-Victorian England. The *Deliverance* gives us the story of reconciliation on the part of a subdued realist who found through acceptance of the City of Man some peace with his lot. As a literary production the *Deliverance* does not maintain the level of the *Autobiography*. It is not that it is less sincere, but that there is less cause for sincerity. The *Autobiography* painted a bold picture of a soul in distress. It centered on perhaps the most intense experience that ever happened, at least imaginatively, to Hale White. The *Deliverance* presents the aftermath. Possibly it possesses the weakness of a sequel. The subject matter is not always so grippingly personal. This may be the reason, too, that the narrative does not flow so smoothly as does the former one. The *Autobiography* never makes us conscious of a story. Here we are somewhat abruptly interrupted in the midst of Mark's London life, are taken into new surroundings, with new characters—the story of Miss Leroy. The decrease of ease also appears on the intellectual side. The thinking seems less an immediate growth from experience, involves us less in progressive discovery. At the same time, the *Deliverance* contains some of Hale White's sharpest realism, his finest vignettes of life in Victorian London. But, if the flame falters on occasion in this novel, it comes back vigorously in his next one, *The Revolution in Tanner's Lane*; and it continues to burn evenly in the three novels that follow after that.

## CHAPTER 4

# *Politics and Religion:*
# The Revolution in Tanner's Lane

THE soaring spirit and the enduring one are celebrated in this novel. They are defined under harassment from a world that is both petty and brutal. The movement of the story arises, somewhat as in the *Deliverance*, from the search for a *modus vivendi* in a society that is unhinged from the forthright faith of its fathers. In this novel the social gospel that substitutes for the aggressive religion of the earlier Puritan radicals fumbles toward programs of political redemption.

The narrative itself is broken into two distinct parts. In the first the action converges on an abortive uprising of the Manchester poor under the inexperienced direction of their intellectual leaders; it is reminiscent of nineteenth-century British socialism in general and of Chartism in particular. (Hale White's own pamphlet, *An Argument for an Extension of the Franchise*, echoes in its very title the chief political aim of the Chartists.) In the second half of the story, the action centers on clerical skulduggery in a provincial world of an emasculated Dissent. Nonconformist zeal, which in the first part is quite as fierce as its theology, is here satirized in its degenerate form of Victorian respectability, a snobbish clergy having deliberately cut itself off from its roots in the common people.

Spiritual sterility is in this novel presented as the negative counterpart of "enthusiasm." The Romantic emphasis on the nobility of great emotion, of dauntless energy and gusto is evident throughout. The *Revolution* is suffused with the spirit of Byron and Carlyle. In his essay, "Byron, Goethe, and Mr. Matthew Arnold," Hale White reveals his allegiance to these ideals. "Energy, power is the one thing after which we pine in this sickly age. . . . Strength is what we need, what will heal us.

Strength is true morality and true beauty."[1] And in another essay, "The Morality of Byron's Poetry," he says, "We do not understand how moral it is yield unreservedly to enthusiasm, to the impression which great objects would fain make upon us. . . ."[2] The sympathetic characters in the *Revolution*, whether Puritans or atheists, share this morality of the natural aristocrat. In them Hale White has embodied that aspect of human nature which already in the *Autobiography* he singled out, when Mark Rutherford confided that he was drawn to those people who "had in some form or other an enthusiastic stage in their history."

The themes of this novel are all closely interwoven, one with another. To be alive means to be engaged, to lead insurrections against privilege. Emotional coldness, especially in women, and its concomitant intellectual shallowness blight human, and especially marital, relations. In both the women and the men it leads to the insipidities of conventional religion, its hypocrisy, and its vaporish gentility. These themes make a continuous pattern through this otherwise divided book. Strictly, there is little plot, though there is much action. This a picaresque novel of the spirit, consisting of a series of improvizations on its main themes. The voice of the author is heard often in direct addresses to the reader, never, however, clashing with the mood being developed, but finely tuned to the drama at hand.

## I  *The First Generation*

The story opens on a scene of popular welcome to Louis XVIII, who has been called back to the French throne. Amidst the shouting multitude on that April morning in 1814 there was one man at least, Zachariah Coleman, who did not cheer "and did not lift his hat even when the Sacred Majesty appeared on the hotel steps. He was a smallish, thin-faced, lean creature in workman's clothes; his complexion was white, blanched by office air, and his hands were black with printer's ink." Such is the unpromising material from which, for Hale White, the heroic virtues arise. As his greatest creation, Zachariah is to embody Hale White's ideal for this world, the heroism of the commonplace. That is why he is introduced so appropriately against the backdrop of meretricious royal ceremony. When he is attacked by the beery, loyalist mob, a certain Major Maitland, aristocratic and republican, comes to his rescue. The two become friends, and Zachariah joins a radical organization headed by the Major and called "Friends of the People." Here Zachariah, nonconformist that he is, finds his natural habitat. Social protest is but another, more direct, manifestation of his credo, the Protestant and democratic conviction of human dignity. "Zachariah had some self-respect," Hale White observes of him when later in the story he is shown trudging from door to door in search of a job, even as the author had himself done on his arrival in London; "he was cared for by God, and in God's book was a registered decree concerning him. These men treated him as if he were not a person, an individual soul, but an atom of a mass to be swept out anywhere, into the gutter —into the river."[3]

The Society of Friends is fired by the principles of the French Revolution; it bears some resemblance in fact to the Society of "Jacques" in the *Tale of Two Cities*, as also does the most significant personage in it whom Zachariah is to know: M. Caillaud, shoemaker, recalls M. Defarge, shoemaker. (Even the later popular uprising seems an echo of the uprising in the Dickens' story.) "Here's your health, gov'nor and d——n all tyrants," is the greeting of a "comrade" when the Major first brings Zachariah to a secret meeting. In reviving the period of early Reform in the second decade of the century, Hale White is being faithful to the spirit of the times, the rebelliousness and the exultation which found its inspiration in the French Revolution. It was the spirit which, for example, possessed Shelley, impelling him to write his "Ode to the West Wind" and, more explicitly, his "Song to the Men of England" and "The Mask of Anarchy" all in 1819 on the occasion of the Manchester Massacre of that year, the prelude to which, the March of the Blanketeers from Manchester in 1817, is the subject of the first half of our novel. In his "Notes on Shelley's Birthplace," Hale White remarks concerning the temper of Shelley's day: "It is important to remember that the French Revolution, or rather *the* Revolution, was on that day the one great fact of Europe, and that Shelley and the Revolution were contemporary, for in him the Revolution breaks out into song."[4] Though the "Revolution" in the title of our novel refers immediately to a minor event in the second half—a small-town skirmish "in Tanner's Lane"—the word has for Hale White large associations, and it applies as well, one cannot but sense, to the theme of revolutionary unrest which runs through the first part. In an essay entitled "Our Debt to France," Hale White makes explicit his connotations for the word: "What is the meaning of Revolution? Externally it is political, but it is more than that. It is the reference of all institutions to first principles, to man. . . . All life at such a season wears a new aspect, the earth again becomes exquisite, heaven infinite, and hence arises a new language and hitherto undiscovered melodies."[5]

The romance of revolution builds its illusion at the opening of this novel. The cathartic thoroughness of especially the French Revolution—which stirred the imaginations of men so various as Carlyle, Wordsworth, Shelley, and the early English socialists— is not unlike that of Hale White's own nonconformist radicalism. The Society of Friends is a group of "ordinary men and women . . . drunk with the beauty and majesty of the new world revealed to them." The aspirations of the English radicals are however to have an outcome different from that of the earlier French enthusiasts. The tale that Hale White has to tell derives from the sad history of early British Reform. He can, necessarily, see only the bad organization, the impracticality of the leaders, lost in noble and abstract principles. The larger curve of slow constitutional development, which in England contrasted so sharply with the aftermath of the French Revolution, is hidden from him. The March of the Blanketeers, on which the political action of the novel pivots, was only too obvious a failure from beginning to end. On March 10, 1817, a group of workingmen met in St. Peter's Field in Manchester, many with blankets rolled up and tied on their backs, for a march to London in order to start an insurrection. They were dispersed by the military and some were arrested. It is their ardor and their hopelessness that Hale White depicts, his words trembling with controlled fury:

> Respectable Manchester was frightened when the Blanketeers met, and laughed them to scorn when they were dispersed. No wonder at the laughter! What could be more absurd? And yet, when we call to mind the THING then on the throne; the THING that gave £180 for an evening coat, and incurred enormous debts, while his people were perishing; the THING that drank and lied and whored; the THING that never did nor said nor thought anything that was not utterly brutish and contemptible—when we think that the THING

## Politics and Religion: The Revolution

was a monarch, Heaven-ordained, so it was said, on which side does the absurdity really lie? . . . The Blanketeers shivering on Ardwick Green, the weavers who afterwards drilled on the Lancashire moors, and were hung according to law, or killed at Peterloo, are less ridiculous than the Crimean War and numberless dignified events in human history, the united achievements of the sovereigns and ministries of Europe.

Carlyle had in *Past and Present* adopted very much the same tone toward the same situation, sneering at the "advanced Liberal" who advised the English "to believe in God, that so Chartism might abate and the Manchester operatives be got to spin peaceably!"[6] On the surface of Hale White's Carlylean bitterness and eloquence is written the cause for which Zachariah sacrificed his security. His inherited nonconformity made such a sacrifice mandatory. Yet the futility of that sacrifice is bound up with the very same qualities, bred into him by his religion, which led him to make it: the unworldly, moralistic approach as opposed to the shrewd, businesslike approach which organized labor was later to develop. "Zachariah, it will be borne in mind," says Hale White of him, "although he was a Democrat, had never really seen the world. He belonged to a religious sect. He believed in the people, it is true, but it was a people of Cromwellian Independents. He purposely avoided the company of men who used profane language, and never in his life entered a tavern. He did not know what the masses really were."[7]

Zachariah himself, at the beginning of the story, is not of obvious heroic cast. That in a sense is the nature of his heroism: it is submerged. He is so ordinary and meek that his strength appears only by degrees out of the harshness of his experience. Of Hale White's celebration of the commonplace, he is the prime example. His vacillation between the old faith and the new protest and his slow maturation into a sage of noble proportions at the end of the novel constitute Hale White's masterpiece of character delineation. This portrayal is not surprising in view of Zachariah's resemblance to the author, bearing as he does the mark not only of Hale White himself but of Hale White's father. At the same time Zachariah lacks a certain human warmth and natural grace. Though inwardly a poet and easily lifted out of himself by Apollonian fervor, he is ill at ease with others. A very English diffidence marks all his relations, especially those with women and most especially those with his wife. "Isaiah, Milton, a storm, a revolution, a great passion—with these he was at home; and his education, mainly on the Old Testament, contributed greatly to the development both of the strength and the weakness of his character."[8] In Byron, with his lofty style, his scorn for the mean and base, his courage, "root of all virtue," Zachariah finds, as did Hale White, the note that answers that of his own being.

Three strains of drama center on Zachariah: struggle with religious, with political, and, tinging his more abstract concerns, with marital difficulties. On the intellectual side the drama has most strength. The conflict is, in effect, a battle between a centuries-old tradition of faith and the new world. "But, alas," Hale White says of his hero, "he was at least a century and a half too late. He struggled, wrestled, self against self, and failed, not through want of courage, but because he wanted a deep conviction."[9] The wrestle of self against self envelops Zachariah's whole being. The world comes to seem empty and loveless, and this is his affliction. "What could be God's purpose in setting him in an alien world where even his wife was indifferent to him?" He is plunged into a familiar Rutherford gloom. Zachariah's intellect is his difficulty, but also it provides the means of escape from the brunt of his personal trouble. His trouble, in other words, is the basis of his philosophy: "he could connect his trouble with the trouble of others; he could give it a place in the dispensation of things, and could therefore lift himself above it."[10]

The Society of Friends offers Zachariah some release, in human intercourse, particularly with two others, like himself superior and isolated: Jean Caillaud, a Frenchman, and his adopted daughter, Pauline, a waif from the stormy days of the French Republic. Still alight from personal exposure to the French Revolution, they are seeking to ignite its flame in the heavier English atmosphere. Politics is their métier, as religion is Zachariah's. Zachariah himself does take fire from them, revolutionary thoughts being natural to his radical Protestantism. "He was a Dissenter in religion and a fierce Radical in politics, as many of the Dissenters in that day were."[11] What is interesting here is the points of positive contact established between English Dis-

## Politics and Religion: The Revolution

sent and French republicanism, their common emphasis on the human dignity of the lowly.

The two great actions of the novel stem from not only the political rebellion in the first half but the religious rebellion on the part of a natural elite, toward the end of the novel, against the diluted Evangelicism of the Victorian age. Zachariah's Calvinism finds easy accord, not so ironically, with a philosophical rationalism that is indebted to Voltaire and Rousseau. This apparently discordant mingling of the old and the new in radicalism is represented graphically in Zachariah's home when, toward the end of his life, we catch a glimpse of him together with his daughter Pauline (so called after her mother, Pauline Caillaud), entertaining a second generation of troubled radicals: "There were portraits on the walls—nothing but portraits—and the collection at first sight was inconsistent. Major Cartwright was still there; there were also Byron, Bunyan, Scott, Paine, Burns, Mr. Bradshaw, and Rousseau. It was closely expressive of its owners." (These portraits, incidentally, were among the very ones hanging in Hale White's own study.)[12]

What is it that Bunyan and Paine, Mr. Bradshaw (the novel's fiery Calvinist preacher), and Rousseau have in common if not the élan they can lend to even the drabbest existence, their sympathy with human aspirations? They all share the vigor which is the persistent ideal in this novel. For Hale White, the function of the mind is to free the heart. In his progress through the novel Zachariah is not so much losing his religion as finding new areas for its application. The old theology is being made relevant to the contemporary scene of Victorian England. A similar transmutation was, as we shall see later, precisely the nature of Hale White's own religious development. The working class descendants of Cromwell's army are in the *Revolution* imbued with the newer protest of Reform.

The relation between heart and mind, the celebration of human warmth and light, of emotional and intellectual élan is illustrated especially in Zachariah's relations with the two women of his life. In a chapter entitled "The Horizon Widens" Zachariah is introduced to Jean Caillaud, shoemaker, and his daughter, Pauline. Their livable, disarranged little room and the vivacity of their conversation are strange to Zachariah, whose own wife is obsessively tidy and intellectually vacuous. Pauline "had none of that horrible mental constriction which makes some English women so insupportably tedious. The last thing she read, the last thing she thought, came out with vivacity and force, and she did not need the stimulus of a great excitement to reveal what was in her."[13]

Pauline offers Zachariah what Hale White desired in a woman: the intellectual companionship such as formed the basis for his relation with George Eliot. Strength, honesty, fearlessness, freedom from the inhibitions of Puritanism—this is what the Caillauds and especially Pauline represent to Zachariah. There is a symbolic scene which occurs during this first meeting. After the heady conversation and the simple meal, the plates all pushed aside in a heap on the table, Pauline retires for a few moments, then returns transformed in a short dress of black velvet trimmed with red, a red artificial flower in her hair, and over her shoulders a light gauzy shawl. She begins to dance to her father's accompaniment on the oboe:

It was a very curious performance. It was nothing like ordinary opera-dancing, and equally unlike any movement ever seen at a ball. It was a series of graceful evolutions with the shawl, which was flung, now on one shoulder, and now on the other, each movement exquisitely resolving itself, with the most perfect ease, into the one following, and designed apparently to show the capacity of a beautiful figure for poetic expression. Wave fell into wave along every line of her body, and occasionally a posture was arrested, to pass away in an instant into some new combination. There was no definite character in the dance beyond mere beauty. It was melody for melody's sake.[14]

Zachariah is transfixed. He has never seen anything like it, though he has sensed the same *esprit* in his favorite authors. Pauline is an attractive feminine embodiment of the flair and grace that attracted him to the poetry of Byron, the vigor indeed that he felt in his favorite author, whose name, in feminine form, Pauline bears—St. Paul. During the dance she has looked serious, "But it was not a seriousness produced by any strain. It was rather the calm which is found on the face of the statue of a goddess." Pauline and Zachariah recognize in each other the quality they share. During an impassioned paraphrase of St. Paul at a tea party Zachariah later gives for his new friends,

## Politics and Religion: The Revolution

Pauline responds to his intellectual enthusiasm somewhat as he had to her dancing: "To Pauline, Zachariah had spoken Hebrew; but his passion was human, and her heart leapt out to meet him, although she knew not what answer to make."

What is notable is Zachariah's rapid development. In the beginning his faith is unshaken. Then there is a weakening, and an infusion of worldliness. His friendship with the heretical Caillauds is the first symptom. The age has gotten into his blood; he can no longer denounce dancing as a work of the devil: "His great grandfather would have done it beyond a doubt, but Zachariah sat still"—and then "walked home with many unusual thoughts." The new individualism, which is an accompaniment of the new heresy of the age, helps to accomplish the change: "The man rose up behind the Calvinist, and reached out arms to his friends." Then another force of his time pries at his creed—science, in the form of astronomy, Hale White's own speciality. From its attack he can simply find no refuge. "Zachariah was a Christian, but the muscles of his Christianity were now, at any rate, whatever they once may have been—not firm enough to strangle the new terror."[15] Thus, as with Mark Rutherford, Hale White delineates in Zachariah his own spiritual development, his decline from orthodoxy.

When Zachariah got home after his first visit to the Caillaud's, "he found, to his surprise, that his wife was still sitting up. She had been to the weekly prayer-meeting, and was not in a very pleasant temper. She was not spiteful, but unusually frigid." The cold Englishwoman, devoid of sympathy for people or ideas, is in Mrs. Coleman (whom Hale White never calls by her first name) pitted against the lively French one. This canker in Zachariah's life contributes a shade to the dark cast of his thought. Incompatibility is only the obverse aspect of the theme of vitality. It is the absence of life that kills Zachariah's marriage. The inability to share with his wife anything of his intellectual struggle makes that struggle all the more desperate. Through Mrs. Coleman, Hale White presents the debit side of Puritanism, the freezing into conventionality of the ardor and viability of the old religion.

When, for example, Zachariah comes home battered and bloody from his encounter with the loyalist mob in the opening episode of the story, Mrs. Coleman's first thought runs to the disruption in her daily schedule. Toward the end, when Zachariah returns after a long absence, he sees her clearly in a pose which is symbolic of her whole life: "The hair was just as smooth, everything about her just as spotlessly clean and unruffled, and she sat as she always did, rather upright and straight, as if she preferred the discomfort of a somewhat rigid position to the greater discomfort of disarranging her gown." Her home has the rigidity of a museum setting. "She could not sit still if one ornament on the mantlepiece looked one way and the other another way, and she would have risen from her deathbed, if she could have done so, to put a chair straight."[16] Her compulsive tidiness is a symptom of her thwarted humanity.

In his own home, Zachariah reflects while in the intimate disarray of the Caillaud ménage, he "often felt just as if he were in his Sunday clothes and new boots. He never could make out what was the reason for it. There are some houses in which we are always uncomfortable. Our freedom is fettered, and we can no more take our ease in them than in a glass and china shop."[17] The warm current of Zachariah's life is chilled in her presence. The evenings of his life with her are epitomized in one sentence. "It was but eight o'clock, and how to fill up the time he did not know." After his first year of marriage to her, he already "was paralyzed, dead in half his soul and would have to exist with the other half as well as he could. . . . He had immortality before him, in which he thanked God there was no marrying nor giving in marriage."[18] "Oh my hero!" Hale White apostrophizes Zachariah in this connection,

Perhaps somewhere or other—let us hope it is true—a book is kept in which human worth is duly appraised, and in that book, if such a volume there be, we shall find that the divinest heroism is not that of the man who, holding his life cheap, puts his back against a wall, and is shot by Government officers, assured that he will live ever afterwards as a martyr and saint: a diviner heroism is that of the poor printer, who, in dingy, smoky Rosoman Street, Clerkenwell, with forty years before him, determined to live through them, as far as he could, without a murmur, although there was to be no pleasure in them.

This situation is peculiar to Hale White's heroes, patiently enduring the harassment of the sordid, which to their fineness of temper is especially repugnant. Zachariah's loneliness—echoed for him in the twenty-second Psalm, "My God, My God, why hast thou forsaken me?"—and his struggle to understand God's decree are stimulants as effective toward his development as is the vivacious friendliness of Pauline.

## II  *The Second Generation*

This story contains its own sequel. In rapid succession Mrs. Coleman, mercifully, dies; Caillaud is executed for treason for his part in the Manchester uprising; Zachariah is imprisoned for two years; and in a brief summary we are told that he has married Pauline, has a daughter by her, and that Pauline herself has died. This is Hale White's way, unconcerned as he is with "plot," of bringing things to a close.

We are next taken to a new scene and new characters with no necessary connection to the previous setting. Though not logically, the two parts are chronologically related. We are shown in them two successive generations of nonconformists battered by the forces of political and religious doubt. The first generation's is a fierce struggle in a reactionary England and an alien universe; the second offers a weaker, more complacent "dissent" in the somewhat less chaotic industrial world of the 1840's. The tone of the second part consequently differs from that of the first, a difference which is enforced by the contrasting portraits of the representative ministers of the old and the new generation; the forthright, humanly and politically involved Reverend Mr. Bradshaw and his opposite number, the central figure of the sequel, the Reverend Mr. Broad. Just as Mrs. Coleman in her coldness and vacuity represented the obverse of the ideal, so too does Mr. Broad in his snobbery, his withdrawal from the life of his impoverished parishioners.

The setting is the peaceful English village of Hale White's childhood, Cowfold, "not a town properly speaking, but the country a little thickened and congested." The Reverend John Broad, minister of Tanner's Lane Chapel, is soon measured up: "He was, however, not a hypocrite, that is to say, not an ordinary or stage hypocrite."[19] He is, in fact, modeled upon the Bedford minister, the Reverend John Jukes, who had refused to help Hale during his scrape at New College and had angered the

Whites before they left the Bunyan Meeting for good. (The name Broad itself was taken from that of a dissenting minister in Hitchin, a town near Bedford.)[20] He is a caricature of respectability, his role being to mark the capitulation of Puritanism to those philistine forces in society it had originally fought. If there was one thing, according to Hale White, which the real dissidence of dissent did not breed, it was the genteel type. That Zachariah was not so is the chief fault the Broads find in him: "summing up the whole argument, he was not 'considered respectable.'"[21]

Broad is not spared by his author even to the extent Mrs. Coleman was. In his portrait, Hale White's distaste for gentility merges with his antagonism to formalized religion; he satirizes through Broad meaningless conventions in both society and religion, their evasiveness, their dishonesty, their masking of crude appetite and rapacious spirit. "The Reverend John Broad was certainly not of the Revival type. He was a big, gross-feeding, heavy person with heavy ox-face and large mouth, who might have been bad enough for anything if nature had ordained that he should be born in a hovel at Sheepgate or in the Black Country."

It is on the clear issues of politics, however, that Hale White's sharpest satire focuses. Here the evasiveness and hypocrisy of the genteel mind are manifest, revealing its sophistical distinctions between politics and religion. Broad is a Tory in all but name. As George Allen, who in this part of the novel is the representative of the old Cromwellian Dissent, is made to explain when Broad cannot bring himself to vote in favor of the Whigs and Free Trade, the minister "goes against all the principles of the Independents." Counter to this identification of religion with politics runs the cowardly respectability of the new breed of dissenting minister that Broad represents: "As a minister of religion," Broad gives out, "it would be better for him to remain neutral." Instead of leading a revolt against privilege, he erects social barriers between himself and his parishioners. His character is an enlargement on that of Deacon Snale, the satiric butt of the *Autobiography*, who, when Mark sought to purify the town's sewage-polluted water supply, similarly urged that ministers should keep themselves untainted by the concerns of the world. In the heat of an election campaign focused on the issue

## Politics and Religion: The Revolution

of the repeal of the tax on foreign corn which is keeping the price of bread high, Broad delivers a sermon—or a caricature of one—on the need for religion to keep itself untouched by earthly strife: "When Mr. Broad came to the secondly, and to that subdivision of it which dealt with freedom from wordly spots, he repeated the words with some emphasis, 'Unspotted from the world.' Think, my friends, of what this involves. Spots! The world spots and stains! We are not called upon to withdraw ourselves from the world—the apostle does not say that—but to keep ourselves unspotted, uncontaminated he appears to mean, by worldly influence."[23] This is the new "gospel according to Tanner's Lane," insincere in tone, pretentious in phrasing. Zachariah, now a patriarch who presides over the younger generation of radicals and who still burns with his youthful ardor for social justice, gives the answer to such sophistry. Cutting through the circumlocution of Broad, he puts the issue plainly: "I should like to have cheap bread, and what is more, I should like to deprive the landlords of that bit of the price which makes bread dear. . . . I believe in insurrection. . . ."[24] Zachariah is only carrying to its conclusion the social protest that stems from his nonconformity.

As a reminder that the old religious fire has not been completely extinguished in these unregenerate days, there emerges here a counterfoil to the Reverend Mr. Broad in the Reverend Mr. Bradshaw, a surrogate of all the heroic ministers of Hale White's youth. It is precisely on the relation of politics to religion, as crucial in this novel as it was in the previous one, *The Deliverance*, that the difference between Bradshaw and Broad centers. "Although he took no active part in politics," says Hale White of Bradshaw, "he was republican through and through, and never hesitated for a moment in those degenerate days to say what he thought about any scandal."[25] His preaching is marked by the ruggedness of his republicanism, quite unlike the genteel soppiness of Broad's generation: "His discourses were remarkably strong, and of a kind seldom, or indeed never, heard now. They taxed the whole mental powers of his audience, and were utterly unlike the simple stuff which became fashionable with the Evangelistic movement." Hale White is here attacking that very liberalizing of religion, as evinced in the Broad Church Movement, which in his particular way, quite outside any church, he himself illustrates in his own religious development.

Bradshaw's republicanism is related to his fierce insistence on the dignity of the lowly. His theological doctrine of "election" is in practice a moral one of hero worship, the hero always being an aristocrat of nature. "God at any rate is no stickler for hereditary rights," he says in one of those cogent and brilliant sermons with which Hale White often leavens his novels. In this particular one, Jephtha is the hero: "Moreover, it does not follow because you, my hearers, have God-fearing parents, that God has elected you. He may have chosen, instead of you, instead of me, the wretchedest creature outside, whose rags we will not touch. But to what did God elect Japhtha? To a respectable, easy, decent existence, with money at interest, regular meals, sleep after them, and unbroken rest at night? He elected him to that tremendous oath and that tremendous penalty. He elected him to the agony he endured while he was away upon the hills! That is God's election; an election to the cross and to the cry, 'Eli, Eli, lama Sabachthani'!"[26] Bradshaws' theme here is again that of the *Deliverance*—the heroism not of great action but of great and passive endurance. Bradshaw's preaching is in its very style, its hortatory fervor, singularly like Carlyle's, no less than is his basic view of man as a fiery spirit elected by God to rise above his fellows. Bradshaw is but another example of how Hale White weaves his personal and his literary admirations into his characters.

The theme of politics as an expression of religion binds together the two parts of this novel, so different otherwise both in subject and in tone. It imparts a unity to that variety which makes the *Revolution in Tanner's Lane*, as all Hale White's readers agree, an outstanding novel. Here we feel is a view both honest and subtle of the tremendous early decades of the nineteenth century, the period of enthusiasm and reform. The strength of the *Revolution* lies in its truth to the spirit of an age; in its richness of characterization; and in its play of mood, from the passionate seriousness of the first part to the many faceted satire of the second. Zachariah and Broad are the representative types of two contrasting generations. Together with the Mark Rutherford of the first two novels, these are Hale White's great characters. In the novels that are now to follow, Hale White turns from heroes to heroines.

CHAPTER 5

## *Science and Religion:* Miriam's Schooling

IN his first three novels, Hale White was preoccupied with his inherited religion, authoritarian and rational. His protagonists were men, embodiments of the Carlylean hero, aristocrats by nature, submerged in the commonplace and ignoble. The context of their struggle was theological and political. With *Miriam's Schooling* begin a series of novels that turn toward the secular religion which Hale White developed under the influence of Wordsworth. His protagonists here are women. These last three novels reflect both Hale White's alienation from the old faith and his growing distrust of politics.

Nineteenth-century English socialism had not proved an adequate replacement for nonconformist liberalism. Even in the *Revolution* the futility of political action was shown, the abortive march of the Blanketeers resulting only in the arrest of its leaders and the disruption of Zachariah's life. Zachariah himself was not a political activist. He was plagued by personal problems quite as much as are the women of the later novels. In all the novels personal salvation is the quest. Only the terms of its fulfillment gradually change. No longer in the later novels is it a question of man's troubled relation with his God. It becomes now a secular, private search for human love. More clearly than even in the earlier novels, these later ones are psychological in their very structure. Somewhat in the manner of George Eliot, their climax is less a change in the outward circumstances than a change in the soul of the heroine. Indeed the latter usually determines the former.

Unlike the *Revolution*, *Miriam's Schooling* has a simple plot; the overt action clearly traces one continuous line. Cowfold (Bedford) is, together with London, still the locale; but its inhabitants are no longer Dissenters, not even hypocritical ones. Nothing indeed could more eloquently testify to the eclipse of the old religion than that complete indifference which need not even pretend to an interest in the Bible: "It is a fact that in those days in Cowfold the church people, and for that matter the Dissenters too, did not read their Bibles."[1] But though the forms of Dissent are absent, the problems which it helped to formulate are still very much alive. The practical conditions of the moral life no longer viewed in those Calvinistic terms that Hale White thought so effective—sin, damnation, election, and grace—are formulated less precisely, and without reference to a theological system of rewards and punishments, in such more psychological language as despair, fear, self-knowledge, and peace.

The effort to find an enlargement and meaning for blind, limited daily existence in small town or large city is still the theme, whatever phrases, with their implied rationale, are used to express it. The singular feature of this novel is that in his portrait of a simple, uneducated, completely a-religious girl, a type on the surface as far as possible removed from Hale White himself, he has given us one of his most intimate and intense self-revelations. The reason for this may lie in the loneliness and suffering of Hale White during the time he was writing *Miriam's Schooling*. In the closing years of the 1880's, before his retirement in 1892 at the age of sixty, life was especially trying for him: his wife was nearing her death from an incurable disease (she died in 1891); his children were marrying and leaving home; his office responsibilities were growing; and, as the effect of long years of overwork and anxiety, he was afflicted with dyspepsia and insomnia. One escape he found during this period was that of looking through a telescope and becoming absorbed in the nightly magnificence of the heavens.[2] This therapy he adopts for the heroine in this novel. In the action which swells to a powerful climax, Miriam achieves through her study of the stars that magical transformation of human nature which William James identified as "conversion," one of his varieties of religious experience, and one which Hale White exhibits as a similarly "religious" process of merging the self with the universal.

Miriam's "schooling" is thus intrinsically a religious one, as Zachariah's was. She is at the same time the most pagan of Hale White's characters, and one of the most loveable. One senses that

## Science and Religion: Miriam's Schooling

he turned to her with a new kind of zest. (Of all his stories, this was the only one that Hale White in his later years said he remembered.)[3] Not only has she no belief, which is what Hale White means when during one of her bitter trials in London, he observes of her, "she had, in fact, no religion whatever"; but, more basically, she does not formulate her unhappiness, connect it to universal causes; it stays on the emotional level. Her ideas are "spontaneous, and consequently disconnected." Hers is a poetic rather than an analytic mind: "It was odd that she could create Verona and Romeo with such intense reality, and yet that she could not perform such a simple feat as that of portraying to herself the revolution of an inclined sphere." But her mentality is not ordinary. In fact, that is just her trouble. With a "certain freshness in her observation" she is stifled by the intellectual torpor of her world. The fact that she is the daughter of an Italian (sharing with Pauline Caillaud of the *Revolution* what were for Hale White the buoyancy and color of a Latin temperament) has something to do with this. She has nothing of English sluggishness. "Hers was one of those natures—happy natures, it may be said—which hasten always to a crisis," Hale White observes of her during an illness. "She had nothing of that miserable temperament which is never either better or worse, and remains clouded with slow disease for months or years." (One thinks here of the long drawn out illness of Hale White's wife.) Together with this vividness of personality, there is also a certain "bohemianism," that permissive untidiness which Hale White's sympathetic female characters often exhibit.[4]

The key to Miriam's nature, like that to Hale White's own, is honesty. It is this which gives rein to her uninhibited remarks. Her temperament, akin also to that of the George Eliot whom Hale White presented as Theresa in the *Autobiography*, requires straightforwardness at the cost of respectability. "I have often dreamt of an island," she at one point says, "in which everybody should say *exactly* what was in his mind. Of course it would be very shocking." Miriam is a typical Rutherfordian heroine: sensitive, fearless, frank, impetuous, and naturally out of sympathy with her surroundings. The people among whom her lot is cast are, on the one hand, the stolid natives of Cowfold and, on the other, the brutalized workers of Victorian London. Here, again, is the trial of a lonesome soul. "Through all the crowd Miriam walked unsympathetic." Hale White presents her thus on a Cowfold market-day. "She cursed the constitution with which she was born. She wished she had been endowed with that same blessed thoughtlessness, and that she could be taken out of herself with an interest in pigs, pie-dishes, and Cowfold affairs generally."[5]

## I  *Cowfold*

Through the story Miriam's problem is clearly developed, without interruption. In sharp contrast to the previous novel, the narrative is one continuous flow, unbroken even by chapter divisions. The economy of the treatment and the singleness of purpose, both of which characterize Hale White's last three novels, help to concentrate the issue. The plot consists chiefly of four situations which encompass Miriam's attempts to adjust to her world. We meet her first at Cowfold, the daughter of a watchmaker with the unlikely name of Giacomo Tacchi—his parents having mysteriously appeared and settled there at the beginning of the century, an errant foreign strain among the stolid English burghers. Her first words in the story mark her as apart; they are a defense of a poor old farmer, Cutts, who for some reason, probably despair, has set fire to his house and is to be tried for arson. That word is enough to turn all Cowfold against him. The fact that he sold good leather, far from being in his favor, is used against him "as part of his plan to make people believe he was an honest man," as one good wife argues:

"Do you recollect," she proceeded with increasing asperity, as became a Cowfold matron, "as it was him as got up that petition for that Catchpool gal as was going to be hanged for putting her baby in the pond?"

"His father," quoth Mr. Cattle, inclining again to his wife's side, "had a glass eye, and I've heerd his mother was a Papist."

"Well," interrupted Miriam at last, "what if he did set fire to his house?"

They all looked amazed. "What if he did! what if he did!" repeated Mr. Cattle; "why it's arson, that's all."

"Oh, that's saying the same thing over again."

"He'll be transported, that's 'what if he did,'" interposed Mrs. Cattle.

*Science and Religion:* Miriam's Schooling

"I suppose," said Miriam, "he wanted to get money out of the Insurance Office. It was wrong, but he hasn't done much harm except to the office, and they can afford it."

She has the wit to distinguish between realities and labels. Musingly, leaving her company behind, she observes that "Anyhow, he wasn't cruel. I would sooner have hung old Scrutton, who flogged little Jack Marshall for stealing apples till his back was all covered with bloody weals." Miriam seeks out the lawyers in the case, and by means of casuistry and downright lying provides Cutts with an alibi. "Her veracity rested on no principle. She was not like Jeannie Deans [in Scott's *Heart of Midlothian*], that triumph of culture, in whom a generalization had so far prevailed that it was able to overcome the strongest passions and prevent a lie even to save a sister's life."[6]

Giacomo, her father, decides to marry again, and Miriam, for no reason apparent to her, is enraged at the idea. Unconsciously jealous, she is further isolated. She finds that she is tired of Cowfold, and also, according to her London aunt, that she has "vegetated" all along. She moves to London with her brother, Andrew, who works as clerk for their uncle. The unwholesome life of a London back street gradually reduces her to despondency. She falls in love with a rather coarse music-hall singer, whose only response to her love is an attempt to seduce her. Andrew, too, succumbs to the evil London atmosphere. He is a colorless boy, without any of his sister's stamina and originality. He takes to drink and loses his job. Owing to the buffetings and the general wretchedness of London, Miriam is driven to the brink of suicide: "Miriam did not know that her misery was partly a London misery, due to the change from fresh air and wholesome living to foul air and unnatural living."[7]

## II  *A New Religion*

Here is sounded the theme which is soon to dominate the story and clarify its meaning: the Wordsworthian belief in the regenerative influence of nature, counterbalancing the degenerative influence of the city. Hale White's own London experience, as recounted especially in the *Deliverance,* enforced this belief, as did his impressions of the lovely Avon Valley and of Stonehenge, which he visited in 1888, the period in which *Miriam's Schooling* was being written.

This novel closely mirrors Hale White's life during these years, the visit to the Avon Valley being in fact literally incorporated in the story. Miriam is taken seriously ill in London and goes to Stonehenge to recuperate. There, in one of the villages on the Salisbury plain, she imbides new life from the grandeur and delicacy of that countryside—the clear, winding river; the dale with its water, cattle, meadow, and dense woods against the wide, treeless chalk downs beyond; and, right over her, the uncanny power of Stonehenge. This is the first stage in Miriam's spiritual progress, looking out over the illimitable plain of Salisbury into the desert of vast eternity, under the mysterious Druid monument. She here begins to perceive some relationship between herself and the greatness outside her. It is an experience akin to Hale White's own, when under the guidance of Wordsworth he replaced "the God of the Crurch" with "the God of the hills," when "God was brought from that heaven of books," as he puts it in the *Autobiography*, "and dwelt on the downs in every cloud-shadow which wandered across the valley."[8] It was particularly Stonehenge that focused for him "the idea of the transitory passage of generations across the planet," making him "the victim of the shapeless emotion which almost overpowers me as I look at it," as he writes in two different letters after his visit there.[9] What next happens to Miriam while she is sitting under the shadow of Stonehenge, quietly transported out of the little irritations of her life, is a clear token of the moral influence of those pleasures of nature which Wordsworth had delineated in, for example, "Tintern Abbey," pleasures "such perhaps/As have no slight or trivial influence/On that best portion of a good man's life,/His little, nameless, unremembered, acts/Of kindness and of love": "Suddenly, and without any apparent connection with what had gone before, and indeed in contrast with it, it came into Miriam's mind that she must do something for her fellow-creatures. How it came there? Who can tell? Anyhow, there was this idea in the soul of Miriam Tacchi that morning." This experience in Miriam exhibits the essential features of religious "conversion." That Hale White so intends it, he leaves us in no doubt. He cites at this point the classic example of conversion, St. Paul's on the road to Damascus: "It may be urged," he observes,

> that no sufficient cause is shown for Miriam's determination. What had she undergone? A little poverty, a little love affair, a little sickness. But what brought Paul to the Disciples at Damascus? A light in the sky and a vision. What intensity of light, what brilliancy of vision, would be sufficient to change the belief and the character of a modern man of the world or a professional politician? Paul had that in him which could be altered by the pathetic words of the Crucified One, "I am He whom thou persecutest." The man of the world or the politician would evade an appeal from the heaven of heavens, backed by the glory of seraphim and archangel. Miriam had a vitality, a susceptibility or fluidity of character—call it what you will—which did not need great provocation. There are some mortals on this earth to whom nothing more than a certain summer morning very early, or a certain chance idea in a lane ages ago, or a certain glance from a fellow-creature dead for years, has been the Incarnation, the Crucifixion, the Resurrection, or the Descent of the Holy Ghost.[10]

What is interesting here is the *Wordsworthian* aspect of the conversion, for it is this which is to become the dominant feature of Miriam's schooling. Her vitality, or susceptibility, responds to the physical beauty of the place. Her religion, like Hale White's own, is eshetic in character; it involves a sense of that beauty as well as a sense of the universe in relation to herself. In recounting his own religious awakening, Hale White, in the guise of "Mark Rutherford," uses the same St. Paul image. The "Lyrical Ballads," he says, "conveyed to me no new doctrine, and yet the change it wrought in me could only be compared with that which is said to have been wrought on Paul himself by the Divine apparition."[11]

Hale White incorporates in this novel Wordsworth's idealization of the common man together with his religion of nature. All his novels of course celebrate the dignity and strength of humble people. But here especially the minor characters embody, often unexpectedly, the common nobility. In this novel the Romantic peasant has been urbanized and appears in authentic little sketches drawn, one senses, from life. Miriam's landlady in London, Miss Tippit, is such a one. She is a neat little person, her hair "always drawn tightly over her forehead, and with extreme precision under her ears. She invariably wore a very tight-fitting black gown, and as her lips were somewhat tightly set, she was a very tight Miss Tippit altogether. It was necessary for her to be so, for beyond an annuity of £20 a year, she had no means of support save letting her lodgings. She was very good, but her goodness appeared to lack spontaneity. It seemed as if she did everything, and even bestowed her rare kisses, under instructions from her conscience, and every tendency to effusiveness was checked as a crime." Here is the type Hale White frequently presents satirically, nursing his aversion for the stiff, duty-bound English woman. Yet Miss Tippit he presents in the most sympathetic of lights. "She might be snappish, limited, and say ugly things during half the week, but there was something underneath all that which was in communication with the skies."[12] (The harsher satirical note frequently sounded in the earlier novels is considerably mellowed in Hale White's later ones.) During Miriam's illness in London it is Miss Tippit who comes to her rescue, an act of kindness that holds a mortifying irony for Miriam, who has resented the very existence of Miss Tippit and once tried to avoid helping her when the little landlady herself was ill. It is this kind of lesson that the unassuming have to teach Miriam, who lacks something of the human touch. Like Zachariah Coleman, Miriam walks alone. Her development is to proceed from just such contacts, forced on her by circumstance.

### III  *An Alien World*

Under the stimulus of her Stonehenge-inspired mission (that "she must do something for her fellow-creatures"), Miriam returns to London to become a nurse. Again she fails; she is soon asked to leave the hospital. Miriam's life up to this point has been a series of failures daunting a fresh, untamed spirit. In this history she is somewhat like a female counterpart of the young Mark Rutherford of the *Autobiography*. Her frustrations are not phrased in terms of the old theology; in fact they are not phrased at all, but they are nonetheless bitter. She now goes back home to Cowfold for the final and most significant phase of her career, one that will bring her to terms with life, as the experiences of the *Deliverance* brought Mark.

With nothing to occupy her at Cowfold, Miriam is driven, al-

*Science and Religion:* Miriam's Schooling

most as a last resort, to marry a basketmaker, a rather stolid but withal a "gay, innocent creature." Under his rather unpromising and certainly unintentional tutelage her real schooling begins. Didymus Farrow, another unlikely name, is insensitive to the peculiarity of Miriam's mind and character. "Mr. Farrow never understood any suffering unless it was an ache of some kind." Again Miriam, this time a little like Emma Bovary, is in an alien world, with no outlet for her restless energy. She curses her constitution, wishes herself endowed with "that same blessed thoughtlessness" that allows others to be interested in pigs and pie-dishes. What she, like Zachariah before her, hungers for is companionship of the mind; her marriage, like his, is to an alien temperament. While she on one occasion loses herself in Verona with Romeo and Juliet, her husband, a skillful and meticulous carpenter, whittles a monkey that can topple over on a long pole. He, unlike Mrs. Coleman, that earlier insensitive partner in an unhappy marriage, is portrayed sympathetically, a token of the very different course Miriam's marriage is to take from Zachariah's. On this occasion he tries to amuse her by acting the part of the monkey itself. Miriam is alarmed to find that something very much like hatred is beginning to develop in her for this man.

"How was life to be lived?" That has ever been her problem. At last the answer is found, and her husband is the one to help provide it. It brings to fruition the incipient efforts at relatedness that had been stimulated by her earlier contacts with such people as Miss Tippit and Mrs. Joll and had been signalized by her sudden but passing experience of "conversion" at Stonehenge. Unlike Emma Bovary's essentially shallow and desperate maneuverings, and in a characteristic Rutherfordian manner, Miriam's answer comes through an enlargement of all her nature, intellectual, moral, and esthetic; it comes, that is, as a religious development, if we follow Hale White's concept of religion.

### IV  *Astronomy and Conversion*

Two events befall her for which she has been prepared without knowing it by her Stonehenge and London experiences. One afternoon out in the park she meets Mr. Armstrong, the elderly vicar of a neighboring village. His passion is astronomy. He has made his instruments all with his own hands, has even, to the scandal of a genteel parishioner, used the top of his church tower for an observatory, and has caused the simpler parishioners somehow to connect the Heaven of the Scriptures with the science of astronomy. (For these particulars Hale White has drawn upon his memories of boyhood expeditions with his father, who had "supplied" the chapels around Bedford—that at Maulden had a telescope and its meetinghouse was also an observatory.)[13] On this particular day Mr. Armstrong has brought a small telescope along to test its power on a clock eight miles away. Miriam looks through it and is delighted to see the dial quite plainly. When Mr. Armstrong asks her to admire the neat, precise workmanship of the box Mr. Farrow has made for it, she is taken aback to learn anything complimentary about her husband. "She knew that her husband was clever with his tools, but she had never set any value on his labours. Now, however, she was really struck with the well-polished mahogany and the piece of brass let into the lid, and when she heard Mr. Armstrong's praises she began to think a little differently."[14] This is the beginning of her introduction to the nature of both the universe and Mr. Farrow, the two points of reference outside herself which are to alter her perspective.

The Reverend Mr. Armstrong's healing influence on Miriam comes, with some irony, not from the established religion which it is his vocation to teach but from the science which is his hobby. Astronomy has led him to an existential relation with the universe: for him the movements in the heavens are felt in their spatial relationships, not just intellectually acknowledged. This is the kind of imaginative stimulation from another human being for which Miriam has been starved. "'The great beauty of astronomy,' he tells her one night when she and her husband visit his observatory, 'is not what is incomprehensible in it, but its comprehensibility—its geometrical exactitude. Now you may look.' Miriam looked first. Jupiter was in the field. She could not suppress a momentary exclamation of astonished ecstasy at the spectacle. . . . What affected her most was to see Jupiter's solemn, still movement, and she gazed and gazed, utterly absorbed, until at last he had disappeared."

Paralleling Hale White's own experience with his newly acquired telescope during the years he wrote the novel, Miriam

## Science and Religion: Miriam's Schooling

has fallen under a spell. It is now that she begins to turn toward her husband. Mechanically oriented, as she is not, he helps her to visualize the revolution of an inclined sphere and also constructs a delicately adjusted orrery in which the relative velocities of the planets in their orbits around the sun are cunningly maintained. At last, when she sees this in operation, she understands, and she undergoes an awakening similar to the one she experienced earlier at Stonehenge: Obedient "to the impulse, every planet at once asnwered; Mercury with haste, and Saturn with such deliberation that scarcely any motion was perceptible. The Earth spun its diurnal round, the Moon went forward in her monthly orbit. . . . Slowly the moon waxed and waned. Slowly the winter departed from our latitude on the little ball representing our dwelling-place, and the summer came; and as she still watched, slowly and almost unconsciously her arms crept round her husband's waist."[15] Miriam is drawn to her husband at the moment of intellectual perception. This is the characteristic insight of Hale White's novels: the enlargement is of the whole human being, just as the needs were; no part, like the mind, can function independently of the rest. This is really the meaning of Hale White's "anti-intellectualism." Miriam's need for intellectual companionship, which caused her at first to disdain her husband's nonpoetic nature, was only a reflection on one plane of the deprivation she felt in all her associations with life. It was a religious need as Hale White conceived religion. This point is enforced by the Wordsworthian character of Miriam's awakening, which is now further to be made manifest. Exactly as in her earlier experiences, the influence of unspoiled nature, cosmic and human, hastens her "conversion," her sense of happy union with the world and with her husband.

### V  *Regeneration*

The two closing and triumphant scenes of the novel are prepared for in a symbolic experience. (The close of this novel depends much on symbolism for the communication of its peculiarly religious meaning.) One wet and dreary afternoon Miriam is driven out of the house in exasperation at the monkey-tricks of Mr. Farrow. "The sky had cleared, and just after the sunset there lay a long lake of tenderest bluish-green above the horizon in the west, bounded on its upper coast by the dark grey cloud which the wind was slowly bearing eastward. In the midst of that lake of bluish-green lay Venus, glittering like molten silver. Miriam's first thought was her husband. She always thought of him when she looked at planets or stars, because he was so intimately connected with them in her mind."[16]

At last Miriam has been able to relate her poetic imagination to her husband, who until now has, quite unaware, defied her instinctual need. As she turns homeward, she is overtaken by one Fitchew, man-of-all-work, "one of the honestest souls in the place." He is the noble peasant, tied by family bonds for centuries to the soil of Cowfold, and has been taken, including his name, right out of the countryside of Hale White's youth, as an account of him in the *Early Life* indicates.[17] His ancestry is as impeccable for Hale White's purposes here as his character. "An old parson always maintained that the name was originally Fitz-Hugh, but this particular representative of the family was certainly not a Fitz-Hugh but a Fitchew, save that he was as independent as a baron, and, notwithstanding his poverty, cared little or nothing what people thought about him. He could neither read nor write, and was full of the most obstinate and absurd prejudices."

The little interchange that follows between Miriam and Fitchew is in its essence a reproduction of Wordsworth's "Resolution and Independence." The rough, illiterate Fitchew reveals under Miriam's questioning the hardship of his life. He has had no work during the long winter, no sleep because of the noise in his ears, and his little thin-lipped wife is, as Miriam knows, hard as flint; yet it is the wife's parsimony that helps the Fitchew family to survive. Miriam remarks that it is a good thing the wife is what she is, to which Fitchew answers, "Yes, well, I said to myself, after I'd had a cup of tea and something to eat this morning—I didn't say it afore then, though—that it might be wuss. If she was allus a slaverin on me and a pityin' me, it wouldn't do me no good; and then we are as we are, and we must make the best of it." That is all, but the moral of Fitchew's life as recorded on Miriam is impressed upon us in what follows. The parallel between the rough Fitchew and the unpolished, unimaginative man who is her husband as well as the disparity between Fitchew's stoicism in the face of real hardship and her

*Science and Religion:* Miriam's Schooling

own desperation in easier circumstances are not lost upon Miriam. That night she has an adventure of the spirit, not unlike the previous one on the chalk downs of Stonehenge. It pours during the night.

Miriam lay and listened, thinking it would be wet and miserable on the following day. She dropped off to sleep, and at four she rose and went to the window and opened it wide. In streamed the fresh southwest morning air, pure, delicious, scented with all that was sweet from fields and woods, and the bearer inland even as far as Cowfold of Atlantic vitality, dissipating fogs, disinfecting poisons—the Life-Giver.

She put on her clothes silently, went downstairs and opened the back-door. . . . Not a soul was to be seen, and she went on undisturbed till she came to her favourite spot where she had first met Mr. Armstrong. She paced about for a little while, and then sat down and once more watched the dawn. It was not a clear sky, but barred towards the east with cloud, the rain-cloud of the night. She watched and watched, and thought after her fashion, mostly with incoherence, but with rapidity and intensity. At last came the first flush of scarlet upon the bars, and the dead storm contributed its own share to the growing beauty. The rooks were now astir, and flew, one ofter the other, in an irregular line eastwards black against the sky. Still the colour spread, until at last it began to rise into pure light, and in a moment more the first glowing point of the disc was above the horizon. Miriam fell on her knees against the little seat and sobbed. . . . Presently she recovered, rose, went home, let herself in softly before her husband was downstairs, and prepared the breakfast. He soon appeared, was in the best of spirits, and laughed at her being able to leave the room without waking him. She looked happy, but was rather quiet at their meal; and after he had caressed the cat for a little while, he pitched her, as he had done before, on Miriam's lap. She was about to get up to cut some bread and butter, and she went behind him and kissed the top of his head. He turned round, his eyes sparkling, and tried to lay hold of her, but she stepped backward and eluded him. He mused a little, and when she sat down he said in a tone which for him was strangely serious—

"Thank you, my dear; that was very, very sweet."

That scene ends the novel. The starry heavens, the sweet countryside, the noble peasant have all served their purpose. Miriam is shown, for once only and at the very end, in a warm, demonstrative action. She has achieved the only kind of salvation a Rutherfordian hero can, a release of stifled faculties—emotional, esthetic, intellectual. Hale White establishes the identification of husband and nature with the indirection of good art. From this final experience of conversion we are left to infer Miriam's final achievement, her acceptance of the world and of her husband.

The pattern of Miriam's development is similar to that of Hale White's earlier protagonists. After the purgatory of the *Autobiography*, Mark Rutherford found in the *Deliverance* a reconciliation with the world and happiness in marriage to Ellen, a woman he had formerly contemned. For Zachariah Coleman of the *Revolution*, Pauline Caillaud offered release from that repressiveness of life which his first wife symbolized. After her own miseries, Miriam finds release through a combination of influences both outside and within her marriage. In all three cases the pattern has been one of negation followed by affirmation, one of death and rebirth. In the two novels that follow this one we shall witness a further development of the motifs and patterns here. *Miriam's Schooling*, though short and unpretentious, is the most seminal of Hale White's later novels.

This story is also a case history in support of Hale White's "anti-intellectualism." Miriam's "schooling" is kept pure of any taint of the academic. In the depths of her misery, she has only her innate arsenal to help her, "with no weapons and no armour save those which nature provides." "She was not specially an exile from civilization," her author goes on to say, "churches and philosophers had striven and demonstrated for thousands of years, and yet she was no better protected than if Socrates, Epictetus, and all the ecclesiastical establishments from the time of Moses had not existed."[18] Miriam's conversion to happiness at the end, moreover, is of greater importance than her comprehension of the physical universe; the intellectual act has significance in so far as it serves a moral end. The value of astronomy is a humanistic one for Miriam, even as it was for Hale White himself.

## CHAPTER 6

## *Love and Religion:*
## Catharine Furze

IN all Hale White's novels the protagonist retraces, as did Bunyan's Christian in *Pilgrim's Progress*, some part of the journey the author has covered. *Catharine Furze*, published the year after Hale White's retirement and also soon after the death of his wife, devotes itself especially to his past, that part of it which preceded his marriage and his arrival in London. He returns here to the scenes he loved most. Bedford, with its willow fringed river, its wharfs and barges, its illimitable distances of sky and land, rises with a bloom that none of his other novels achieves. Catharine herself is the spirit of the place, the most poetic of his creations. She is like one of those girls in Botticelli's "Primavera," an allegorical representation, almost impersonal, of the youth of the world. The symbolism which proliferated toward the end of *Miriam's Schooling* is here further developed. The course of Catharine's story, its crises and solutions, are conveyed largely through the scenic features, the farm that was the lost Eden of Hale White, the peaceful river and its bridge.

In its essentials, Catharine's story is the only one Hale White has to tell. It is another version of the struggle of Mark and Zachariah and Miriam, that of the exceptional nature which must suffer in isolation for its gifts, its heroic quality finding release in that embrace of the whole universe which characterizes the religious experience. With Catharine this theme is highly individualized. She is like quite no other of Hale White's protagonists, a young girl growing suddenly into womanhood, clear and unspoiled to the end. She develops under the stimulus of love. Her lover is a minister who is married. It can be seen that Hale White is pressing his theme into the most difficult mold. To make the relationship of a young girl to a married man, and he her minister, serve as a vehicle for the disclosure of the true nature of religion, and while doing that to prevent those worldly-wise asides reserved for the term "Platonic," would tax any novelist, not to say a Victorian one. May it be said to Hale White's credit as a man of sensibility that never once in the course of the story does he lose his hold. He is himself so possessed by his theme and his tone is so steady and strong that the reader surrenders to it. This novel is a triumph of tact. It maintains that tension between expectation and fulfillment which is the mark of the expert. Hale White is not a master craftsman in the manipulation of the "plot," but he is one in the disclosures of the spirit. In *Catharine Furze* his main concern is always also the reader's: how these two exceptional people, caught in the web of society, may for a moment or two in their lives illustrate his theme, that of the true nature of religion.

## I  *The Enemy at Home*

In the opening pages Hale White gives us the Bedford scenes and characters of his childhood with a solidity and precision unmatched in his earlier work: the ancient town on the fens by the banks of a broad, slow-moving river, with its six-arched stone bridge; the elm-lined High Street leading off into three or four narrow lanes, and centering on the churchyard; just beyond the church, going from the bridge along High Street, the market place with its cattle pens, the Bell Inn opposite the Moot Hall, and the bow-windowed shops. The year is 1840, the generation that of the Reverend John Broad of the *Revolution*. Mr. Furze, largest ironmonger in Eastthorpe, and "a most respectable member of a Dissenting congregation," exemplifies the new Dissent. "He was not a member of the crurch, and was never seen at the week-night services or the prayer-meetings.... The days were over for Eastthorpe when a man like Mr. Furze could be denounced, a man who paid his pew-rent regularly, and contributed to the missionary societies."[1]

In this context is to be reënacted the drama of the freedom loving spirit, constricted and forced in upon itself. Mr. Furze's daughter, Catharine, is, like Miriam, sensitive, intelligent, and strong-willed. Her need to communicate is even greater than was Miriam's. Catharine does not know what she wants until it

*Love and Religion:* Catharine Furze

is too late: after she has been overwhelmed by love. Then she begins to understand herself a little. To this she is helped by almost all the obstacles in her life, and first of all by her mother, who is her natural enemy. Mrs. Furze represents just those features of Eastthorpe which drive Catharine to revolt. Mean spirited, self-centered, and hypocritical, Mrs. Furze embodies the unpleasantest qualities of Mrs. Coleman and the Reverend Broad. Her first thoughts are always of appearances; to these she is willing to sacrifice her daughter and her husband. Her horizon can be gauged from the nightmarish vision she conjures up on the presumption, quite erroneous, that her daughter is bent on marriage to their apprentice, Tom Catchpole. "What! won't you have a word to put in about her marrying a fellow like that, your own servant with such a father?" she says to her husband, who never can marshall reasons against his wife to defend the actions toward which his instincts correctly guide him.

"And how are they to live pray? Am I to have him up here to tea with us, and is Phoebe to answer the front door when they knock, and is she to wait upon him, him who always goes down the area steps to the kitchen? I do not believe Phoebe would stop a month, for with all her faults she does like a respectable family. And then, if they go to church, are they to have our pew, and is Mrs. Colston to call on me and say, 'How is Catharine, and how is your son-in-law?' And then— oh dear, oh dear!—is his father to come here too, and is Catharine to bring him, and is he to be at the wedding breakfast? And perhaps Mrs. Colston will inquire after him too. But there, I shall not survive that! Oh! Catharine, Catharine!"[2]

As part of her campaign to rise to the social level of the brewer's wife, Mrs. Furze persuades her husband to move from their home above his ironmonger shop, symbol of Puritan industry and frugality, to the pretentious neighborhood of the "Terrace." On the occasion of their moving, Hale White allows us a glimpse of that middle-class taste which he so abhorred and which, in the train of his own many movings from house to house, led him to write that denunciation of the tawdriness of the contemporary stuccoed houses that Ruskin printed in *Fors Clavigera.*[3] After this a change in religion would be appropriate, a transfer from chapel to church. Mrs. Furze's argument is "that the people who go to church are vastly more genteel, and so are the service and everything about it—the vespers—the bells—somehow there is a respectability in it." She accomplishes the transition by donating Mr. Furze's money freely for those "renovations" that Hale White, with his taste for simplicity and authenticity, detested as much as he did all vulgarity. "The builder undertook 'to give the pipe outside a touch of the gothic, so that it wouldn't look bad,' and as for the other stoves, there were two windows just handy. By cutting out the head of Matthew in one, and that of Mark in another, the thing was done, and, as Mrs. Colston observed, 'the general confused effect remained the same.'"[4]

Mr. Furze, reluctant in all these projects is tractable in his wife's hands: "he was a victim in that unhappy dread of a quarrel which is the torment and curse of weak minds." But with Catharine it is a different matter. Mrs. Furze knows her daughter's strength. She fears even to announce the change of domicile and so lies to Catharine. Catharine's opinion of the Terrace, and of nearly everything Mrs. Furze represents, she expresses in no uncertain terms: "I hate it. I detest every atom of the filthy, stuck-up, stuccoed hovel." Hers again is thus the trial of incompatibility, the burden the heroic natures in Hale White's stories have to bear, usually in the marital but here in the parental relation. It is a trial of integrity by native dishonesty, which for Hale White is the inward sign of "respectability." In order to get rid of Tom Catchpole, for example, Mrs. Furze bribes a fellow worker of Tom to fabricate a charge of larceny against him. She operates deviously, gaining her ends always by insinuation. Refusing to reflect on her actions, she has the added advantage of a clean conscience. It is this kind of dishonesty which for Hale White is the mark of the weak generation, allowing it to desert the stern and binding faith of the past for one more genteel. "It is, perhaps, more correct to say that the word deception has no particular meaning for them," Hale White observes of the type Mrs. Furze represents.

The development of Mrs. Furze's character is as pertinent to the theme of this novel as is that of Catharine. She embodies all that for Hale White is negative. She also provides the irritant necessary to her daughter's growth. For Catharine retains the temperament if not the faith of the old breed. She has the hunger of Zachariah and of Mark for an understanding of herself

*Love and Religion:* Catharine Furze

in relation to the universe. There are passages expressing her condition which could have been taken right out of the *Autobiography*:

How impatient she became of those bars which nowadays restrain people from coming close to one another! Often and often she felt that she could have leaped out towards the person talking to her, that she could have cried to him to put away his circumlocutions, his forms and his trivialities, and to let her see and feel what he really was. Often she knew what it was to thirst like one in a desert for human intercourse, and she marvelled how those who pretended to care for her could stay away so long: she could have humiliated herself if only they would have permitted her to love them and be near them.

Standing by herself, she seems to be "an individual belonging to no species, as far as she knew."[5]

## II  *Minister and Lover*

Catharine's particular situation is like Miriam's, but it is developed in a different way. Not precisely fitting into the rôle of polite young lady set for her by Mrs. Furze, Catharine is sent to a school to be "finished." Instead it is her inner life that here undergoes a revolution. She comes to the school alive with "spiritual activity," the last thing for which such a school provides. Her problem is to get outside herself as her predecessors in Hale White's novels have done. The outlet she finds is in neither science nor faith nor social work, but in Mr. Cardew.

The Reverend Mr. Cardew, the rector at her school, gives as it were public expression to her private problem the first time she hears him preach. It is a sermon somewhat like Mark Rutherford's first, one of those eloquent reinterpretations of the old doctrine into which Hale White pours his own convictions. Cardew's text is from Luke XVIII, 8: "And a certain ruler asked Him, saying, Good Master, what shall I do to inherit eternal life?"

Mr. Cardew did not approach his theme circuitously or indifferently, but seemed in haste to be on close terms with it, as if it had dwelt with him and he was eager to deliver his message.

"I beseech you," he began, "endeavor to make this scene real to you. A rich man, an official, comes to Jesus, calls Him Teacher—for so the word is in the Greek—and asks Him what is to be done to inherit eternal life. How strange it is that such a question should be so put! how rare are the occasions on which two people approach one another so nearly! Most of us pass days, weeks, months, years in intercourse with one another, and nothing which even remotely concerns the soul is ever mentioned. Is it that we do not care? Mainly that, and partly because we foolishly hang back from any conversation on what it is most important we should reveal, so that others may help us. Whenever you feel any promptings to speak of the soul or to make any inquiries on its behalf, remember it is a sacred duty not to suppress them."

In these words Cardew articulates Catharine's inmost need, the same one Miriam had, for that serious intellectual companionship which is opposed to the frivolous, sterile intercourse Catharine has come to despise in her mother and the provincial snobs her mother courts. For the first time in her life Catharine hears words which speak to her directly. She is profoundly moved. "Such speaking was altogether new to her; the world in which Mr. Cardew moved was one which she had never entered, and yet it seemed to her as if something necessary and familiar to her, but long lost, had been restored."[6] Mr. Cardew is one like herself, "a creature who speaks the veritable reality and wakes in us the slumbering conviction of universal imposture." Cardew himself recognizes Catharine as one of the elect. He too is isolated by an "entirely interior life," and "prone to self absorption." He is another one of Hale White's partial self-portraits. Cut off from his wife, who inhabits the world he rejects, he finds in Catharine the only opportunity for communication. He in her, and she in him, find exactly the communion each wants, the honesty and seriousness which breaks through the conventional into the real. A meeting such as theirs, Hale White emphasizes, is rare in our time: "the world as it is now is no place for people so framed. When life runs high and takes a common form men can walk together as the disciples walked on the road to Emmaus." And so their love, with its human and physical basis, partakes of the nature of a religious communion.

That the elements which combine to give their love its peculiar quality are quite well understood by Cardew, have in fact been imaginatively anticipated by him, is clear from a story of his own composition that he one day gives Catharine to read. It

## *Love and Religion:* Catharine Furze

tells of a certain Charmides, a sculptor living in Rome in the fourth century. Greek by birth, fastidious in his taste, he was imbued with all the culture of the pagan world. With his heightened sense of beauty and his unconscious need for an all-embracing goal in life, he was indeed very much like the hero of Pater's *Marius the Epicurean* (published in 1885, eight years before *Catharine Furze*). But he was also very much like Hale White's own heroes, seeking like them release—both Platonic and romantic—in the imaginative world of the ideal. Once he was rewarded when viewing a statue of Pallas Athene that he had just completed, "severe, grand in the morning twilight . . . no inanimate mineral mass but something more. . . . Part of the mind which formed the world was in it, actually in it." He despised the barbaric crudity of the Jewish sect, their irrational belief in miracles, their savage god, "a boor upon a mountain, wielding thunder and lightning."

One day he wandered into one of their hovels, where extracts from letters by a certain Paul addressed to the sect in Rome were being read, the strangest jargon about justification and sin. Roman women were there, lovely but cold. He noticed the excitement on the somewhat common features of a slave girl, Greek like himself, and his curiosity was aroused. Some days later he met this girl again, and recognizing him she gave him a copy of the letter to take home. As he read it, this Palestinian manuscript, full of superstition and supernaturalism, seemed rude to him in comparison with the classical sanity of such an author as Lucretius. But the face of the girl kept returning to him while he was reading, and he could not stop. What finally converted him was his falling in love with the slave girl, "but it was a love so different from any love which he had felt before for a woman, that it ought to have had some other name. It was a love of the soul, of that which was immortal, of God in her: it was a love, too, of no mere temporary phenomenon, but of reality outlasting death into eternity. There was thus a significance, there was a grandeur in it wanting to any earthly love. It was the new love with which men were henceforth to love women—the love of Dante for Beatrice." They were betrayed after coming from one of their underground meetings and though Charmides was given a chance to exculpate himself, he chose to die with his loved one, "For Christ and the Cross."[7]

The title of this story by Cardew is "Did He Believe?" It is a parable whose meaning is the theme of this novel. When Charmides admired in his statue "the mind which formed the world," "the Divine idea which was immortal," he was being prepared for the experience which was to follow, the transformation of a rational, emotionally unsatisfied "pagan" to a "believer," one, that is, imaginatively engaged with life, so much so that he would die for his belief, or at least for his emotional ties. The impetus for his conversion was supplied by love. Charmides indeed could never distinguish between his love and his faith and that is why, as Cardew added at the end, he was never considered a martyr by the Church: "The circumstances were doubtful, and it was not altogether clear that he deserved the celestial crown." This doubt on the part of orthodoxy, conveyed by Cardew in the title of his story, measures the difference between the old doctrine and Hale White's reinterpretation of it. For Charmides, love itself was a religious communion; it was "different from any love which he had felt before for a woman," "a love of the soul, of that which was immortal, of God in her." It was truly Platonic and Dantesque, a human love fused with a divine one.

When he wrote the words just quoted above, Cardew was, before the event, rendering in the symbolic language of Christianity the experience he was now having with Catharine. Hale White is at pains to identify the kinship among all those imaginative experiences which find expression in love and religion and art. These, all experiences of newness, of rebirth, are opposed to the aridity represented by Mrs. Furze, whose function in the novel is to define its theme through contrast. Catharine represents its affirmation:

> Catharine was one of those creatures whose life is not uniform from sixteen to sixty, a simple progressive accumulation of experiences, the addition of a ring of wood each year. There had come a time to her when she had suddenly opened. The sun shone with new light, a new lustre lay on river and meadow, the stars became something more than mere luminous points in the sky, she asked herself strange questions, and she loved more than ever her long wanderings at Chapel Farm. This phenomenon of a new birth is more often seen at some epochs than at others. When a nation is stirred by any religious movement it is common, but it is also common in a different shape

during certain periods of spiritual activity, such as the latter part of the eighteenth century and the first half of the nineteenth in England and Germany.[8]

Here lies the focus of Hale White's insight and the particular contribution he has to make to fiction: his understanding of one kind of human relationship. "She was in love with him"—he says of Catharine's relation to Cardew—"but what is love? There is no such thing: there are loves, and they are all different. Catharine's was the very life of all that was Catharine, senses, heart, and intellect, a summing-up and projection of her whole selfhood."[9] A cogent example of the union of senses, heart, and intellect has already been provided by Miriam, who under the intellectual stimulus of astronomy was able to develop a love for nature and a love for her husband. With regard to Catharine, Hale White enforces his point by remarking that had she known them, Shakespeare or Wordsworth might have helped her. What drew Catharine to Cardew was as much the world of poetry as the man. "Whether it was the preacher's personality, or what he said," Hale White observes of her response the first time she hears Cardew preach, "Catharine could hardly distinguish, but she was profoundly moved. Such speaking, was altogether new to her; the world in which Mr. Cardew moved was one which she had never entered, and yet it seemed as if something necessary and familiar to her, but long lost, had been restored."[10]

### III  *The Outsiders*

Cardew is a married man, but, Hale White makes it clear, not "a canting, hypocritical parson." The man is inconsistent, it is true, as Hale White adds, "inconsistent exactly because there was so much in him that was great." He has lived much within himself; his standards lack the perspective of one who mingles much with others. He has a habit of making people uncomfortable by the sudden, naïve introduction of intimately held convictions. "Once even, shocking to say, he quite unexpectedly at a tea party made an observation about God."[11] This high seriousness bears the Rutherfordian stamp. Cardew's is the heroic temperament of Mark, Bradshaw, Zachariah, and, back of them, of Bunyan and the Apostles, of the time when a man could without the possibility of embarrassment ask of another, "What shall I do to inherit eternal life?" But until he meets Catharine,[12] he can ask such questions only in his sermons, which are both intensely personal and grandly universal.

With his wife he cannot communicate, again in true Rutherfordian fashion. She lies outside his dimension, though she tries hard to reach him. Mrs. Cardew is indeed a pathetic figure. Anxious to please her husband, she arranges with Catharine a little reading from Milton in order to improve her understanding, but this only irritates Cardew when he finds out about it. Hale White is careful to draw a sympathetic portrait of the wife here, unlike his portrait in the *Revolution* of Mrs. Zachariah Coleman, who personified the principle of negation somewhat as does Mrs. Furze in this novel. Mrs. Cardew's is another kind of heroism, silent and patient. She cannot put into words her feelings about either her husband or Milton, and this Cardew finds unpardonable.

Mrs. Cardew partakes of the primitive and appealing simplicity of some of Hale White's other characters, like Mrs. Joll in *Miriam's Schooling*. There is another person of this sort here, and he completes the central foursome of two initiates in and two aliens from the realm of the spirit to which this novel is dedicated. This fourth one is Mr. Furze' apprentice, Tom Catchpole. Each of the aliens would like to gain entrance to the realm, not for its own sake, not because he belongs there, but for the ulterior purpose of gaining the affection of one of the initiates: Mrs. Cardew of her husband; Tom of Catharine. It is this utilitarian approach to an area and a relation that is the antithesis of the utilitarian which initially and finally excludes them.

Tom has gradually superseded his master in the management of the ironmonger's shop. He is adept in practical matters, but "the spiritual world was non-existent for him." Recalling the character of another outsider, Mr. Farrow, husband of Miriam, Tom cannot understand mental suffering; "he could not comprehend why a person should be ill when there was nothing the matter."[13] The single emotional attachment in Tom's life is Catharine. And just as Mrs. Cardew has sought out Catharine for help in reaching her husband, so Tom, with equal irony in a

## *Love and Religion:* Catharine Furze

symmetrically parallel situation, seeks out Cardew for help in reaching Catharine. Each of the outsiders recognizes a spiritual deficit, a world of mystery that is somehow closed off; each wants the same kind of initiation. Tom wishes he too could be ill without a reason, so that he might partake of this secret life. Catharine respects Tom's probity and capability, sensing what neither of her parents can recognize, that Mr. Furze's business depends completely upon Tom's shrewd management. But she cannot love him. "One penetrating word from Mr. Cardew thrilled every fibre in her, no matter what the subject might be. Tom, in every mood and upon every topic, was uninteresting and ordinary." In one of the great scenes of the novel, Tom goes in his need to Cardew. He and Catharine have just been listening to a sermon by Cardew on the prodigal son,[14] in which the minister has dwelt on the wonder of irrational tenderness. "Oh, my friends," said the preacher, "just consider that it is this upon which Jesus, the Son of God, has put His stamp, not the lecture, not chastisement, not expiation, but an instant unquestioning embrace, no matter what the wrong may have been. If you say this is dangerous doctrine, I say it is here. What other meaning can you give to it? At the same time I am astonished to find it here, astonished that priest-craft and the enemy of souls should not have erased it." That "instant unquestioning embrace, *no matter what the wrong may have been,*" lends biblical sanction to impulsive tenderness such as Catharine and Cardew feel for each other, and this is not lost upon Catharine. After the sermon Cardew, his wife, and Catharine are all very much excited. Tom has been watching Catharine closely, noting her eager, rapt attention, and then following her out of the church, felt the electricity in the air around the Cardews and Catharine. He is agonized by his exclusion from their world. As Mr. Cardew walks slowly down Rectory Lane to the river, Tom sets out after him. At the boat landing, he seats himself by Cardew's side, and there in the light of the full moon they see a lady appear and then disappear on the opposite bank. It is Catharine, of course, in search of Cardew, as Cardew is there in the hope of meeting her. At this point Cardew is in a great hurry to leave, but Tom, intent on his own purposes, keeps him there and begins to question him about his sermon.

"What you said about the Mediator was true enough, but somehow, sir, I feel as if I ought to have liked the first part most, but I couldn't, and perhaps the reason is that it was poetry. Oh, Mr. Cardew, if you could but tell me how to like poetry!"

"I am afraid neither I nor anybody else can teach you that; but why are you anxious to like it? Why are you dissatisfied with yourself?"

"I do not think I am stupid. When I am in the shop I know that I am more than a match for most persons, and yet, Mr. Cardew, there are some people who seem to me to have something I have not got, and they value it more than anything besides, and they have nothing to say really, really, I mean, to those who have not got it, although they are kind to them."

"It is not very easy to understand what you mean."

"Well, now to-night, sir, when you talked about God moving in us, and the force which binds the planets together, and all that, I am sure you felt it, and I am sure it is true, and yet I was out of doors, so to speak."

"Perhaps I may be peculiar, and it is you who are sane and sound."

"Ah, Mr. Cardew, if you were alone in it, and everybody were like me, that might be true, but it is not so; it is I who am alone."

"Who cares for it whom you know? You are under a delusion."

"Oh, no, I am not. Why there—there." Tom stopped.

"There was what?"

"There was Miss Furze—she took it in."

"Indeed!" Mr. Cardew again looked straight on the ground, and again scratched it with his stick.[15]

The world that Tom cannot fathom is that of religion as Hale White understands it, the world of imagination and poetry. It is, in Tom's paraphrase, "God moving in us, and the force which binds the planets together." That Tom has some inkling of this, his love for Catharine would indicate. "To Tom, Catharine was miracle, soul, inspiration, religion, enthusiasm, patriotism, immortality, the fact, essentially identical, whatever we like to call it, which is not bread and yet is life." But beyond immediate love he cannot go. And if there is one point Hale White has to make it is that the immediacy of love acquires significance only as it is assimilated to a greater universe by the imagination and so becomes a religious experience. This is of course where Tom fails, and it is this which gives the love of Catharine and Cardew its peculiar intensity.

## Love and Religion: Catharine Furze

Hale White is consistently successful, while building up the approaches of Cardew and Catharine toward each other, in avoiding the clichés of the triangular situation (Mrs. Cardew being the third party) in which he has put them. In spite of the obvious dangers of this situation, considering Cardew's position and Catharine's innocence, there is never a slip into the stereotypes of an "affair." Not that Hale White scants the physical side of the relation, as far at least as Cardew is concerned, though he does with regard to Catharine in accordance with his Victorian attitude toward girlish innocence. In depicting Cardew, he makes it clear that the very force which moves his imagination and makes him truly religious is also physical in nature. "Vitality means passion," he says.

Because of his physical awareness perhaps, because he is the older one, and certainly because he is the man, Cardew is the more aggressive and the less cautious of the two. "Undoubtedly he was drawn to Catharine because her thoughts were his thoughts. St. Paul and Milton in him saluted St. Paul and Milton in her.[16] But he did not know where to stop, nor could he look round and realize whither he was being led."[17] No word of endearment, however, ever escapes the lips of either Cardew or Catharine when they are together. Their talk is always on impersonal matters. Hale White is hewing true to the line he has established in his earlier novels. His concern is not with another love story and the rough course it must run, but with human loneliness and the search for that understanding which is ultimately religious. Tom's case illustrates this, as does also Mrs. Cardew's. Both seek to win their loved one by somehow acquiring a sense for poetry. Tom naïvely asks Cardew how to go about liking it. Mrs. Cardew, somewhat more sophisticated because she has lived with the problem for a longer time, tries to elicit the sense from Catharine during the little seminars on Milton. The function of both Tom and Mrs. Cardew in the story is thus to underscore the kind of understanding which is the basis for Cardew's and Catharine's love.

That it is really understanding Cardew seeks, that he is not just rationalizing a passion, Hale White makes clear a bit later. After Tom, Mrs. Cardew wanders down the path to the river, where she comes upon her husband: "Mrs. Cardew took her husband's hand in her own sweet way, kissed it, and held it fast. At last, with a little struggle she said—" 'My dear, you have never preached—to me, at least—as you have preached to-night.' " This is the first time she has evinced any of that kind of understanding Cardew needs, and also for the first time in the novel Cardew is able to show her some affection, even though it is somewhat clouded by his feelings for Catharine. "You really mean it?" he says. "She kissed his hand again, and leaned her head on his shoulder. That was her reply. He clasped her tenderly, fervently, more than fervently, and yet! While his mouth was on her neck, and his arms were around her body, the face of Catharine presented itself, and it was not altogether his wife whom he caressed."

Another irony of the relationships in this story is that each of the two initiates, Catharine and Cardew, is forsaking his natural partner for the life of the imagination each finds in the other. It is a case of the freedom of the spirit against the bonds of the world. In this respect it is the story of Zachariah Coleman and Pauline Caillaud over again. On his way home from the river Tom meets Catharine on that eventful night, and under the stimulation of his interview with Cardew blurts out to her his love. Upon hearing this, Catharine, silent for a time, at last says: "My dear Tom." And "Tom shuddered at the tone."

For Catharine life is over. Her refusal of Tom brings vividly before her that her remaining days will be spent without love since she rigidly represses her natural impulses toward Cardew. The result is that her temporary solution in her inner surrender to Cardew has only exacerbated her original problem—her need for communication—as well as produced a new conflict. She is possessed by thoughts of death, a prey to the black desolation that few of Hale White's heroes escape. As she wastes away, a very different man from Cardew takes charge.

### IV  *The Physician: Reality and Death*

That Hale White is not wholly satisfied with the theme that has dominated the novel, the superior claims of the life of the imagination over the more mundane ties of life, is indicated by his introduction of this new type of character toward the end and by the ending of the novel itself. Dr. Turnbull, Catharine's

## Love and Religion: Catharine Furze

physician, is a "materialist." Like Edward Gibbon Mardon, who in the *Autobiography* attacked Mark's religion, he is skeptical of what religion, in Hale White's context, represents. He is presented as the antithesis of Cardew. His ministrations to Catharine resemble those of a modern psychiatrist. About Cardew he observes to her that he is "a remarkable man in many ways, and yet not a man whom I much admire. He thinks a good deal, and when I am in company with him I am unaccountably stimulated, but his thinking is not directed upon life. My notion is that our intellect is intended to solve real difficulties which confront us, and that all intellectual exercise upon what does not concern us is worse than foolish."[18] He is calling Catharine back to reality, away from that world of the imagination that she shared with Cardew and that caused both her love and her mental suffering. The problems of a Cardew, he warns Catharine, "are to a great extent artificial, and all the time spent upon them is so much withdrawn from the others which are real. He goes out into the fields reading endless books, containing records of persons in various situations. He is not like any one of those persons, and he never will be in any one of those situations."

Though this attack on Cardew's imaginative life would in its implication invalidate all literature, including Hale White's own novels, its immediate effect on Catharine is of course salutary. She has lost hold of reality in her romantic pursuit of an unattainable ideal. This is what the doctor understands. "Every thought which maims you is wretched," he tells her. He attacks also another romantic notion to which Hale White himself subscribes, one which indeed lies at the core of all his fiction, the exaltation of the superior person, the natural aristocrat. "Nothing is more dangerous, physically or mentally," he admonishes his young patient, "than to imagine we are not as other people. Strive to consider yourself, not as Catharine Furze, a young woman apart, but as a piece of common humanity and bound by its laws. It is infinitely healthier for you. Never, under any pretext whatever, allow yourself to do what is exceptional. If you have any originality, it will better come out in an improved performance of what everybody ought to do, than in the indulgence in singularity." To enforce this point, which also runs counter to all the implications Hale White has been developing in this novel, Dr. Turnbull launches into an encomium of the realism and practicality of Mrs. Cardew, the heroine, as he conceives her, in their midst: "While he is luxuriating amongst the cowslips," he says of Cardew, "in what he calls thinking, she is teaching the sick people patience and nursing them. She is a saint, and he does not know half her worth."

In his handling of Dr. Turnbull, Hale White makes more explicit a curious ambivalence that has been lurking in his attitude toward Cardew and the subject of marriage. Though Catharine is blameless, we are not so sure of Cardew, who has allowed his passion to overrun his obligations as a husband. Hale White does not himself seem so certain in this novel about his old *bête noir* of incompatible marriage. The doctor, definitely a sympathetic character, is made to enlarge on the moral duty of a husband to love his wife. Hale White's own wife had died after a long illness just before he published this novel. A parallel between Cardew's indifference to his ailing wife and Hale White's own life is possible here. The inference would seem to be that through Dr. Turnbull, Hale White is voicing his own second thoughts and private regrets on this subject. Dr. Turnbull is the advocate Hale White felt was needed to present the case against that quest for the ideal and often disembodied life which is the persistent theme of his fiction. The reflection of his own experience, of his own regrets, in his picture of the Cardew marriage may help to explain not only the more moderate tone Hale White takes toward the theme of incompatibility here but also the frequent defenses he makes of the pedestrian partner, Mrs. Cardew, even while sympathetically showing Cardew's alienation from her. The problems of marriage are less clear-cut for him now than they were in the earlier novels, his understanding is deeper, and his presentation is accordingly more convincing.

With the way barred in every direction for Catharine, the story spins to a rapid conclusion. Catharine, actually the more self-controlled of the two in her relation with Cardew (it is she that always ended their interviews, usually by jumping up and running away) is the real sufferer in this triangle, and its eventual victim. Cardew begins to see the wisdom, or at least the inevitability, of Catharine's restraint. "As he went along something came to him—the same Something which had so often restrained Catharine. It smote him as the light from Heaven smote Saul of Tarsus journeying to Damascus."[19] Again the St. Paul image is

*Love and Religion:* Catharine Furze

used by Hale White to signalize a conversion, this time to holy matrimony. Cardew turns to his wife, awakened into recognition of merits he has not suspected in her, somewhat as Miriam at the end of the preceding novel turned to her husband. Thus both by her stimulation and then by her self-abnegation has Catharine altered Cardew's life and character. He is "saved" by her, as he tells her later. Catharine, too, has been changed, has been able to extend herself out to other people, as her solicitous care for a dying servant girl, shortly before her own death, indicates. On Catharine's deathbed she and Cardew for the first and only time in the novel intimate their love to each other. The admission is couched in the language of their religion:

> "Mr. Cardew, I want to say something."
> "Wait a moment, let me tell you—*you have saved me.*"
> She smiled, her lips moved, and she whispered—
> "*You* have saved *me.*"

And Hale White comments: "By their love for each other they were both saved. The disguises are manifold which the Immortal Son assumes in the work of our redemption."[20] In this way the theme of the novel has once for all been given. Love has here been so deeply involved with religion that it has in fact become one of its "disguises."

CHAPTER 7

# *Philosophy, Love, and Religion:* Clara Hopgood

APPROPRIATELY, *Clara Hopgood* is the last novel that Hale White was to write; it presents conclusively, though from a new vantage, the pervasive theme which has been growing through his fiction—that the intensity of the relation between two gifted and isolated people is an experience indistinguishable from that of religion. This time there are two heroines, two sisters. The flexibility afforded by such double concentration allows Hale White to play unusual variations on his theme. Broadly, two situations are developed. In the first part of the story, the absence of intellectual sympathy between the two lovers, who have everything else to help them—physical attraction, social approval, money—tears them apart before they are married, even though a child is to be born to them. In the second part, the lovers have little *except* intellectual sympathy to hold them together, yet because of it, one success is dramatically crowded upon another.

Madge and Clara Hopgood are unlike any other of Hale White's heroines—cultivated, articulate, self-possessed, aware of themselves and of the world; they sound in fact at times like characters in a Shaw play. Their father has been "peculiar in his way of dealing with his children. He talked to them and made them talk to him and whatever they read was translated into speech; thought, in his house, was vocal."[1] For their education he sent them to Germany, the center for the "seething ferment" of thought in the early days of the century, as Hale White recalls in his *Autobiography*.[2] At Weimar the girls had been stimulated by the poetry of Goethe, the music of Beethoven, the rationalism of the *Leben Jesu*. Back at Fenmarket they felt suffocated. In his sallies against the "dulness and complete isolation from the intellectual world" of the small town in Victorian Eng-

*Philosophy, Love, and Religion:* Clara Hopgood

land, Hale White reveals an animus not unlike that of Sinclair Lewis against its American counterpart of a later day. The provincial mentality which Hale White so sharply satirized in the Mrs. Furze of his previous novel is again attacked.

But here the slant is significantly different. This novel is to develop into a pro-feminist one, a defense of the "new woman," growing out of a tradition which reaches back to Milton's *Doctrine and Discipline of Divorce* (1643), to Mary Wollstonecraft's *A Vindication of the Rights of Women* (1792), to Mill's *Subjection of Women* (1869), a tradition that culminated in Hale White's own day in Ibsen's *A Doll's House*, to which play *Clara Hopgood* has unusual affinities. In all these works, the humanism of the Renaissance and the Reformation, which had tacitly been reserved for men only, is extended to include women as well. Mill's description of the ideal marriage reads like a statement of the burden of Hale White's fiction: "marriage in the case of two persons of cultivated faculties, identical in opinions and purposes, between whom there exists that best kind of equality, similarity of powers and capacities with reciprocal superiority in them." It is the "conversation meet" of Milton's more succinct phrase which *Clara Hopgood* celebrates. The intellectual vacuity is the Victorian norm for the good woman that Hale White attacks. When he turned from the men of his three first novels to the women of his last three, he changed only one facet of his theme. His women have the same intensity of thought and feeling as his men; are given to speculation; are faced with similar problems; are presented, in short, as those unique aristocrats of nature that Hale White finds buried in the most ordinary rounds of life. The difference between his earlier heroes and his later heroines is that the problems of the women are couched always in terms of human relations rather than in terms of the old creed. Fundamentally, these women are faced with the same challenge as were the men: to find the law of their own nature; to find how to live their lives with dignity, at peace with themselves, to find, in other words, "salvation" in the modern world.

### I  *The New Woman*

When we first see Clara and Madge, they are playing chess. "Check," says Clara after only about a dozen moves. She is the controlled and rational one. Madge cannot contain herself. "The moment I go beyond the next move my thoughts fly away, and I am in a muddle and my head turns round," she says. Madge lacks that faculty of the scientific imagination, the ability to visualize a change of positions and all its coordinated rearrangements, which is usually associated with men and is taken as a sign of strength. It is this very faculty that Miriam developed under the stimulus of astronomy and that gave her the strength to carry on with a life that had been falling to pieces. Clara has this faculty. "I should like to be a general," she says, "and play against armies and calculate the consequences of maneuvers."[3] A little later she says, in words that are prophetic, "You are very much mistaken if you suppose that, because of one failure, or of twenty failures, I would give up a principle." Madge sweeps all the chess pieces into the box and defends impulse, including love at first sight, with all the vigor of a romantic and unhurt nature.

Frank Palmer, the son of a London drug manufacturer, interrupts the girls' conversation when with an Ibsen-like entrance, he alights from the London coach under their window. Madge meets him soon after and, with that facility at beginnings and endings which marks Hale White's plots, they are lovers almost at once. Madge clearly demonstrates her dependence on impulse. Then second thoughts intervene. The difficulty is that with all his physical attractiveness to her, which sweeps away most of her doubts when she is in his presence, he has nothing beyond that to offer her. He is, as Hale White describes him, "not particularly reflective, but he was generous and courageous, perfectly straight-forward, a fair specimen of thousands of English public school boys."[4] That last mass identification indicates Hale White's role for him. He belongs outside the circle of initiates, one of those, like Mrs. Cardew and Tom in the preceding novel, who seek to enter the circle only for the ulterior purpose of gaining access to a loved one living within it. There is a colloquy between Madge and Frank on the subject of Tennyson very like that of Mr. and Mrs. Cardew on the subject of Milton:

"I do greatly admire Tennyson," he said.
"What do you admire? You have hardly looked at him."
"I saw a very good review of him. I will look that review up again, by the way, before I come down again."

## *Philosophy, Love, and Religion:* Clara Hopgood

It is basically because of this approach to Tennyson that Madge determines not to marry Frank, and thereby to destroy her reputation; for she knows she is to bear him a child. Frank, however, is intoxicated. Brought up as a "pure" young man, he for the first time "found himself the possessor of a beautiful creature whose lips it was lawful to touch. . . ." Like Tom Catchpole in his relation with Catharine Furze, he realizes that there is a deficiency in him somewhere. "There was something undiscovered in Madge, a region which he had not visited and perhaps could not enter." Rather touchingly, he sets about memorizing a long poem to demonstrate his love of poetry. He chooses the right poet but unhappily the wrong poem, Wordsworth's "Intimations of Immortality," (which Hale White regarded as one of Wordsworth's weaker poems, damning it in *The Athenaem*: "it is desultory, will not stand examination . . . by the reason," and lacks simplicity).[5]

In rejecting Frank, Madge opens herself quite knowingly to suffering; and suffer she does, as only Hale White's characters can. When Frank learns that he is to be the father of her child, he likewise is distraught. He pursues Madge, not primarily because he loves her but because of a fear for his own reputation and a profound sense of insecurity, "a strange horrible trembling such as men feel in earthquakes when the solid rock shakes, on which everything rests."[6] Madge is now, however, acting on something stronger than impulse: her schooling for salvation of the only kind Hale White allows his heroic characters, the salvation of integrity and independence. "Whatever wrong may have been done, marriage to avoid disgrace would be a wrong to both of us infinitely greater,"[7] she writes to Frank. Madge adopts a course which even for our time is drastic.

For her Victorian world this sacrifice of her worldly fortunes for a higher principle within herself is even more dramatic. "I know what you are going to say," she answers Frank on one occasion when he catches her and pleads with her. "I know it is a crime to the world; but it would have been a crime, perhaps a worse crime, if a ceremony had been performed beforehand by the priest, and the worst of crimes would be that ceremony now." There speaks the voice that in Milton and in Mill upheld the sanctity of marriage as a sanctity of the union of spiritual equals above all else.[8] In Madge speaks also the voice of the "new woman" who in the Victorian Age is the popular exponent of these avant-garde views of the past. She, the "wronged" one, rejects the man, and the old cliché is further distorted when it is the man who pleads for marriage.

Small wonder that Hale White's friends were dismayed and that the novel aroused a minor furor in the press. W. R. Nicoll, his warm admirer, described the novel in the *British Weekly* of July 9, 1896, as "unworthy" of him, its "moral teaching . . . in sad contrast with that of his earlier books." Hale White felt it necessary to defend himself in the same periodical three weeks later, on July 30, "against the charge of immorality brought against *Clara Hopgood*. The accusation is another proof," he adds, "that even in a country which calls the New Testament a sacred book, the distinction between real and sham morality is unknown."[9]

Madge's refusal to marry Frank is a protest against the double standard of sexual morality, an assertion of an individuality within herself just as precious as any man's. Ibsen's *A Doll's House* was presented to the English public in 1889, seven years before the publication of *Clara Hopgood*. And in 1891 Bernard Shaw in the *Quintessence of Ibsenism* had declared that women are the slaves of duty; men assume such servitude on their part, both men and women clinging to the pretense that self-sacrifice for men is women's natural medium of expression. The slight public furor over *Clara Hopgood* was an echo of the storm which had broken over the first English production of Ibsen. In both cases the cause of the public indignation was the paradox, as Shaw put it, of placing duty to oneself above duty to one's family. Madge is a Nora who, instead of leaving a man she cannot respect, refuses to marry one by whom she has a child, a Nora taking a greater risk in behalf of the principle of self-determination in Victorian society. Here the girl who "got into trouble" refuses to be made "an honest woman."

As another irritated reviewer put it about *Clara Hopgood*: "To marry the man who should have been the husband for her child becomes a crime if they cannot agree upon matters of literary taste," and adds that it never occurred to Madge that she was neglecting her duty to her child as well as to her mother and sister.[10] But all this neglect only emphasizes Hale White's major concern with honesty and dignity. He chose to stress this point;

## Philosophy, Love, and Religion: Clara Hopgood

its costs in other respects could fall where they would. The irony of course is that for Madge dignity lies in becoming a "fallen woman." This indicates her complete reversal of conventional standards. Madge realizes the uniqueness of her demands and of her position. Hale White presents her with tenderness even as he presents Frank with sympathy. But, though her struggle is severe, her determination is unshaken.

Madge's refusal of Frank is also a protest against that kind of incomplete marital relationship which Hale White in so many different ways depicted with ridicule and disgust. A stroke of genius in this novel is that Frank is not made a villain or a trifler but just an average good fellow. This norm is exactly his fault in a Rutherfordian sense. Madge, who is above average, will not live with what to her would be a vacuum. The punishment visited by an irate society is for her as nothing compared to the desolation of an incompatible union, one that will continually frustrate her spiritual need. Her refusal to compromise with honesty to the man and with dignity for herself had been already anticipated in Hale White's first novel, when Mark Rutherford refused to marry his childhood sweetheart, Ellen, though all the social conventions urged him to do so. This theme of honesty to self at all costs is central in all Hale White's work. It appeared at the beginning of his *Autobiography*, as it did at the beginning of his own life, in Mark's refusal, analogous to Madge's, to succumb to the social pressure put upon him to become a minister, a refusal he defended in his old age: "I might have succeeded in being content with a *mush* of lies and truth, a compound more poisonous than lies unmixed, but I was enabled to resist. . . . I can see now that if I had yielded I should have been lost forever.[11]

### II  Counterparts in Love and Philosophy

Except for one indirect comment when, against all their convictions, she tests Madge's strength of purpose by playing the devil's advocate—suggesting that perhaps Madge is expecting too much of herself and of Frank—virtually never in all Madge's trouble does Clara interfere. Instead she and their mother, putting their own lives to the side, quietly quit their comfortable Fenmarket home for the dirt, the unfriendliness and the poverty of London. These discomforts, like the scorn of a society flaunted, are considered by them as negligible compared to the danger of living a life untrue to oneself.

In London, Clara finds work as a bookseller's assistant. When she meets an elderly gentleman, Baruch Cohen, the second episode of the novel begins. Baruch has very little to offer Clara except the most important quality of all, a harmony emanating from a central unity of his nature and radiating to all he says and does. "In nothing was he more Jewish," Hale White says of him,

> than in a tendency to dwell upon the One, or what he called God, clinging still to the expression of his forefathers although departing so widely from them. In his ethics and system of life, as well as in his religion, there was the same intolerance of a multiplicity which was not reducible to unity. He seldom explained his theory, but everybody who knew him recognised the difference which it wrought between him and other men. There was a certain concord in everything he said and did, as if it were directed by some enthroned but secret principle.[12]

Baruch is one of the great ones, unsurpassed by any other of Hale White's characters. This superiority may well be owing to the closeness of identification here between author and character. Isolated by age and race (as was Leopold Bloom in *Ulysses*), Baruch is essentially like Hale White in his spiritual eminence and in his sense of social inadequacy. "He often made advances," Hale White says of Baruch; "people had called on him and had appeared interested in him, but they had dropped away." The same kind of despairing observation about himself in the guise of Mark Rutherford, Hale White had made in the *Deliverance*: "We went out of our way sometimes to induce people to call upon us whom we thought we should like; but, if they came once or twice, they invariably dropped off, and we saw no more of them. This behaviour was so universal that, without the least affectation, I acknowledge there must be something repellent in me, but what it is I cannot tell."[13]

The portrait of Baruch reflects also Hale White's life-long veneration for Spinoza, whose *Ethic* he had translated over thirty years before. Baruch's attitude is contemplative; his is the intellectual's withdrawal from life. "I am not fitted for such work," he says of the feasibility of his joining a political movement; "I have

## Philosophy, Love, and Religion: Clara Hopgood

not sufficient faith. When I see a flag waving, a doubt always intrudes. Long ago I was forced to the conclusion that I should have to be content with a life which did not extend outside itself."[14] But Baruch's is also, more spectacularly, the intellectual's triumph over life. In earlier novels, Zachariah and Miriam have illustrated the therapeutic power of ideas. Baruch shows how ideas can generate a new mode of existence, a completely human and civilized one.

One Sunday morning he was poring over the Moreh Nevochim, for it had proved too powerful a temptation for him, and he fell upon the theorem that without God the Universe could not continue to exist, for God is its Form. It was one of those sayings which may be nothing or much to the reader. Whether it be nothing or much depends upon the quality of his mind.
There was certainly nothing in it particularly adapted to Baruch's condition at that moment, but an antidote may be none the less efficacious because it is not direct. It removed him to another region. It was like the sight and sound of the sea to the man who has been in trouble in an inland city. His self-confidence was restored, for he to whom an idea is revealed becomes the idea, and is no longer personal and consequently poor.[15]

Baruch, who bears Spinoza's Hebrew name (of which "Benedictus" is the Latin equivalent), seems to be a projection of Hale White's renewed interest in the philosopher during the years he was at work on *Clara Hopgood*. This novel was published in 1896, and between 1892 and 1894 Hale White was occupied with a second preface (in reality a long commentary) to his translation. Baruch's life history resembles that of Spinoza. Like the philosopher, he is a lens maker; his father came from Holland, Spinoza's native land. Even the name of Clara, whom Baruch is to love but not to marry, is the same as that of the girl, Clara van den Ende, who refused to marry Spinoza.[16] Also, like Spinoza, Baruch finds in mathematics the "foundation" of the universe. In any event, whatever these biographical resemblances may mean, Hale White has put into Baruch's words some of his most trenchant observations. The isolation which is the affliction of Baruch's life is also the token of its greatness. Hale White speaks from the depths of his own isolation when he remarks of Baruch: "He had no friends, much as he longed for friendship, and he could not give any reasons for his failure. He saw other persons more successful, but he remained solitary. Their needs were not so great as his, for it is not those who have the least but those who have the most to give who most want sympathy."[17]

In Clara, Baruch recognizes a familiar spirit. Theirs is the instant meeting and, out of their need, the instant love. Both Clara and he are startled inwardly at the ease with which each can advance from the retreat deep within the self to communicate with the other. Baruch finds in Clara not merely a sympathetic listener who can relieve his loneliness, not only an interesting young girl who appeals to his passion, but an equal to whom he can communicate his thoughts. His intellectual appetite as a matter of fact augments his love:

> His tendency to reflectiveness did not diminish his passion: it rather augmented it. The men and women whose thoughts are here and there continually are not the people to feel the full force of love. Those who do feel it are those who are accustomed to think of one thing at a time, and to think upon it for a long time. "No man," said Baruch once, "can love a woman unless he loves God." "I should say," smilingly replied the Gentile, "that no man can love God unless he loves a woman." "I am right," said Baruch, "and so are you."[18]

The quality of the Cardew-Catharine relationship is again apparent. The experience of love is like that of religion. We can now gauge more clearly the negative function of Madge's affair with Frank. Where Frank had everything to offer except this quality, Baruch has *nothing* to offer except it. In each case it is just this conjunction between the love of a woman and the love of God that makes all the difference. We may here recall also the story of Miriam, for whom love was so closely interwoven with the operations of the universe. The fact that Baruch thinks like Spinoza, for whom God and the universe are the same, makes it possible for him to coalesce those experiences of love and religion and cosmic understanding which have been brought so closely together in Hale White's two preceding novels. Here even more forcefully the physical passion is stimulated by the intellectual kinship. Immediately preceding Baruch's total capitulation, his falling in love with Clara "suddenly and totally," Clara has spoken to him "with the ease of a person whose habit was to deal with principles and generalizations," and in her talk he can discern her recognition of the "One in the many." This sudden

*Philosophy, Love, and Religion:* Clara Hopgood

intimacy of Clara and Baruch derives from the shared secret common to all Hale White's heroic characters, that initiation into a mystery of personal and cosmic relationship that Tom Catchpole and Mrs. Cardew ruefully recognized as beyond their horizon. This alone is requisite. After one of their walks together, in the course of which she has sensed the electrical impulse of Baruch's attraction, Clara, back at home, "lay down without any misgiving. She was sure he was in love with her; she did not know much of him, certainly, in the usual meaning of the word, but she knew enough."[19]

### III  *The Greater Sacrifice*

For all the similarity of this relationship to that in *Catharine Furze*, the two people here are subtly and interestingly different from their earlier counterparts. Especially is this true of Clara. She is no love-struck girl but a woman whose strong-willed adherence to principle has in the course of her history been amply demonstrated. Her feeling for Baruch seems to be almost rationally motivated. This is the woman who strengthened Madge's determination to reject Frank because "each person's belief, or proposed course of action, is a part of himself, and if he be diverted from it and takes up with that which is not himself, the unity of his nature is impaired and he loses himself."[20] Clara's response to Baruch comes from her realization that he represents the unity of her own nature. "Clara was not as Baruch" (for whom "it was hair, lips, eyes, just as it was twenty years ago").

In spite of her attachment, however, her judgment guides her behavior. If love should come to her, she said in her opening conversation with Madge, "I should try to use the whole strength of my soul. Precisely because the question would be so important, would it be necessary to employ every faculty I have in order to decide it. I do not believe in oracles which are supposed to prove their divinity by giving no reasons for their commands."[21] Her decision is made now, on quite rational grounds, against herself:

A husband was to be had for a look, for a touch, a husband whom she could love, a husband who could give her all her intellect demanded. A little house rose before her eyes as if by Arabian enchantment; there was a bright fire on the hearth, and there were children round it; without the look, the touch, there would be solitude, silence and a childless old age, so much more to be feared by a woman than by a man. Baruch paused, waiting for her answer, and her tongue actually began to move with a reply, which would have sent his arm round her, and made them one for ever, but it did not come. Something fell and flashed before her like lightning from a cloud overhead, divinely beautiful, but divinely terrible.[22]

What "fell and flashed" before her has to do with her sister, whom Baruch has not yet met. At this climactic moment Clara determines her course of action, and she never falters. She manipulates circumstances so adroitly to bring Baruch and Madge together that we are reminded of her skill at chess and of her opening remark that she would like to be a general and "calculate the consequences of maneuvers." For the light that flashed upon her revealed Baruch's special appropriateness for Madge, the spiritual kinship possible in a marriage of these two whom she knew so well. Clara's lack of response in the last interchange between them, when she began the process of eliminating herself from the picture, Baruch can ascribe only to his own personal failure. He goes home to a dead fire; as far as he can see, his last chance to begin a new life has disappeared.

Madge sacrificed marriage for the sake of her own integrity; Clara sacrifices it for something even greater. Never is this concept put into words. In a scene which point for point corresponds to the climactic one at the end of *Miriam's Schooling*, where Miriam wordlessly comes to terms with her life and her husband, Clara comes to her decision. Both scenes are symbolic: an early morning initiation rite, quietude, the freshness and sweetness of the countryside just after rain, the clouds driven by a southwesterly wind into a bank above the eastern horizon, the miracle of sunrise, tears, catharsis, resignation, peace in a decision made:

Clara, always a light sleeper, woke between three and four, rose and went to the little casement window which had been open all night. Below her, on the left, the church was just discernible, and on the right, the broad chalk uplands leaned to the south, and were waving with green barley and wheat. Underneath her lay the cottage garden, with its row of beehives in the north-east corner, sheltered from the cold winds by the thick hedge. It had evidently been raining a little, for the drops hung on the currant bushes, but the clouds had been

*Philosophy, Love, and Religion:* Clara Hopgood

driven by the south-westerly wind into the eastern sky, where they lay in a long, low, grey band. Not a sound was to be heard, save every now and then the crow of a cock or the short cry of a just-awakened thrush. High up on the zenith, the approach of the sun to the horizon was proclaimed by the most delicate tints of rose-colour, but the cloud-bank above him was dark and untouched, although the blue which was over it, was every moment becoming paler. Clara watched; she was moved even to tears by the beauty of the scene, but she was stirred by something more than beauty, just as he who was in the Spirit and beheld a throne and One sitting thereon, saw something more than loveliness, although He was radiant with the colour of jasper and there was a rainbow round about Him like an emerald to look upon. In a few moments the highest top of the cloud-rampart was kindled, and the whole wavy outline became a fringe of flame. In a few moments more the fire just at one point became blinding, and in another second the sun emerged, the first arrowy shaft passed into her chamber, the first shadow was cast, and it was day. She put her hands to her face; the tears fell faster, but she wiped them away and her great purpose was fixed. She crept back into bed, her agitation ceased, a strange and almost supernatural peace overshadowed her and she fell asleep not to wake till the sound of the scythe had ceased in the meadow just beyond the rick-yard that came up to one side of the cottage, and the mowers were at their breakfast.[23]

Later that morning at the country outing she has arranged, Clara sees Madge and Baruch sauntering by the river. "The message then was authentic," she said to herself. "I thought I could not have misunderstood it." There is yet one more scene, a brief and final one, through which the necessary information concerning Madge's own decision is conveyed. Just before they return to London from their outing, Madge, totally unaware of course of Clara's role, takes Clara aside:

"Clara," she said, "I want a word with you. Baruch Cohen loves me."
"Do you love him?"
"Yes."
"Without a shadow of a doubt?"
"Without a shadow of a doubt."
Clara put her arm around her sister, kissed her tenderly and said,—
"Then I am perfectly happy."
"Did you suspect it?"
"I knew it."[24]

Clara, like Madge before her, is living up to a standard above that of the world. As for Madge, she discovers in Baruch someone who can supply that important element to a human relation that Frank Palmer lacked and there is no restraint in her acceptance of him.

## IV  A Secular Saint

A new character now enters. Rather strangely, it is Mazzini, whom Hale White much admired, and whom he visited when Mazzini was in England. Though at this late point in the story there is little opportunity for the unfolding of his character, Mazzini has in a sense been prepared for. He serves, in the final act of Hale White's last novel, to epitomize all Hale White's heroes—the Carlylean aristocrat, the Romantic enthusiast, the Christian saint, the idealist, the philosopher. Especially does he concentrate the essence of Baruch's greatness. He is the intellectual *par excellence*. His "was not the face of a conspirator but that of a saint, although without that just perceptible touch of silliness which spoils the faces of most saints. It was the face of a saint of the Reason, of a man who could be ecstatic for rational ideals, rarest of all endowments." As with Baruch, ideas are both his nutriment and his religion. This emerges as Mazzini expounds his political philosophy, which is based on the premise that society is founded not "on rights" (the English view) but on duty:

> "To put it in my own language," said Madge, "you believe in God."
> Mazzini leaned forward and looked earnestly at her.
> "My dear young friend, without that belief I should have no other."
> "I should like, though," said Marshall, "to see the church which would acknowledge you and Miss Madge, or would admit your God to be theirs."
> "What is essential," replied Madge, "in a belief in God is absolute loyalty to a principle we know to have authority."[25]

With dramatic irony, Madge is here setting the stage for Clara's last act. The appeal of Mazzini's views to Clara is overwhelming. At her first meeting with Mazzini she is converted to his political faith and out of this conversion grows her percep-

*Philosophy, Love, and Religion: Clara Hopgood*

tion of a way out for herself. This is the Clara who said earlier, "If I were famous, I would sacrifice all the advantages of the world for the love of a brother—if I had one—or a sister."[26] Having given up her earthly love, nun-like she privately takes the vow to reason and duty. Mazzini, also with dramatic irony said in his first words on the girls' visit to him, "The English are a curious people. As a nation they are what they call practical and have a contempt for ideas but I have known some Englishmen who have a religious belief in them, a nobler belief than I have found in any other nation. There are English women, also, who have this faith, and one or two are amongst my dearest friends." Clara exemplifies such a faith. She goes off to Italy, to take up the cause of Mazzini,[27] and there she dies.

And so this has been the story not primarily of Madge's fall, but of Clara's sacrifice that is unknown to the beneficiaries of it, Madge and Baruch. Clara has transferred, quite literally, a love which was rightfully hers, and which she personally needed, to a sister who needed it for her own "unity of nature." It has been the story of the victory of principle over impulse. Clara, like Miriam and Catharine before her, indeed like Zachariah and Mark before them, exhibits the special kind of heroism that Hale White reserves for his finest creations, the heroism of submission, his secular version of saintliness. When the novel as a whole is seen in perspective, Madge's sacrifice of her reputation in the cause of her integrity becomes a prelude to the even nobler sacrifice of Clara in the cause of saint-like charity. This is why the novel is named after Clara rather than after Madge Hopgood, though the love affair of Madge looms larger and is more conventionally dramatic. The unconventionality of this approach seems to have confused even Arnold Bennett, who remarked in his *Journal*, "*Clara Hopgood* is not about Clara Hopgood, but about her sister Madge Hopgood, and Clara is only dragged in at the end."[28]

From a view of the novel as a whole—its moving characterization of a modern saint and its authentic presentation of a twofold drama of human integrity—the charge of immorality against it because of Madge's refusal to enter into marriage under false pretenses even when she was pregnant becomes a ludicrous, vulgar one. It represents the kind of provincial "respectability" that Hale White was striking out against in all his novels and that he satirized so effectively in his portraits of Mr. Snale, the Reverend Mr. Broad, and Mrs. Furze. Hale White could well say in answer to his Victorian critics that "the accusation is another proof that even in a country which calls the New Testament a sacred book, the distinction between real and sham morality is unknown."

CHAPTER 8

# *Themes of the Fiction: The Short Stories*

HALE WHITE'S short stories develop themes made familiar to us by his novels. His heroes are of the world of Zachariah Coleman. Michael Trevanion, for instance, is "fervently religious, upright, temperate, but given somewhat to moodiness and passion. He was singularly shy in talking about his own troubles."[1] The struggle, fierce though it may be, is internal and muted. The exploitation of gloom is distasteful to Hale White, contrary to his tact and to his sense of his art. To become funereal would defeat his presentation of vigorous and even aggressive seriousness. The literature of his time is melancholy, he notes, for example, "because it is easy to be melancholy, and the time lacks strength." He is alive always to any touch of falseness.

Marital difficulties usually provide the context within which the conflicts of his heroes are fought out. In "A Dream of Two Dimensions," one of his cleverest stories, the husband lives in a three dimensional world all by himself. All others live in a world of two dimensions, have no depth, nor can in their shadow realm comprehend what depth means; this applies especially to his wife. The theme of alienation is given another turn in "Michael Trevanion," one of Hale White's most poignant stories, with echoes from Wordsworth's "Michael" and the parable of the Prodigal Son. It is a story that concentrates Hale White's characteristic themes.

Michael, a stonemason, burning with the convictions of the old religion and constricted by all its prohibitions, radiates, with all his limitations, the glory inherent in the common man. "How sublime a thing is this dust or dirt we call man!" his author apostrophizes him. Unhappy in his marriage, Michael vests all his pent-up affection in his son. Yet from this relation too he immures himself because he disapproves of the girl the son loves. Being "of the world," she is "not elect." Michael endures a double misery, not only shut off from the only human being he loves but agonized by the dread that the boy is about to repeat the fatal error of his own unhappy life. "His case was very simple and very common," Hale White remarks of Michael's marriage, "the simplest, commonest case in life. He married . . . when he was very young, before he knew what he was doing, and after he had been married twelve months, he found he did not care for his wife. . . . Michael had never for years really consulted his wife in any difficulty because he knew he could not get any advice worth a moment's consideration"[2]—an exact duplication, this, of Zachariah's lot. Michael's dread of a repetition of such a mistake becomes obsessive, owing to his total identification with his son. "The boy . . . was his father; not only with no apparent mixture of the mother, but his father intensified." Until the very end, the anti-feminine bias in this story is unusually strong. Michael tries to separate the two lovers in full consciousness that his behavior will alienate the boy further and that for the rest of his life he will be irretrievably alone: "he had educated himself to complete self-obliteration for the sake of his child." His suffering unfolds itself in a drama that ends with unexpected irony when the girl in question proves to him her integrity, an ending that serves only to heighten the portrait of Michael's love-starved life.

Love, when it is happy, is never carnal. Hale White's ideal woman is something of a Pre-Raphaelite visitation from another world. In "A Mysterious Portrait" this ideal emerges, though only pictorially so to speak—the two-dimensional motif again—as a mysterious lady for love of whom the protagonist is consumed. He sees her fleetingly, from an unapproachable distance, at widely spaced intervals during his life. He never speaks to her and nobody else with him ever sees her, though always there is some memento of her presence left behind, such as a neckerchief in a coach. At last, toward the end of his life, he finds her likeness in a portrait. He seeks out the painter, only to learn that the original was a private vision. It is a plot that Henry James would have liked.

Indeed, Hale White's theme of estrangement between men and women; his predilection for situations in which love is almost,

## Themes of the Fiction: The Short Stories

but never quite, attained—or if attained is immediately followed by the death of the loved one—closely parallels James's approach. It is probably a result of the same repression of the "lower" passions as with James. Hale White's women are "pure," unearthly, and definitely un-English. The lady of the mysterious portrait is thus described: "a more exquisite face I thought I had never beheld. It was not quite English—rather pale, earnest, and abstracted, and with a certain intentness about the eyes which denoted a mind accustomed to dwell upon ideal objects."[3] In this emphasis on the unearthly quality of his ideal woman Hale White is of course at one with the current of his time. In this respect he antedates the naturalistic approach of the later years of the century.

The repression of the "instinctual life," says Mr. Lionel Trilling, is illustrated in Matthew Arnold's love poetry, which "represents modern man as being deprived of his sexual freedom and energy." This statement is just as true of Hale White's fiction. The "fear of the loss of the power to feel," Mr. Trilling notes, "this is one of the great themes of the literature of the last century and a half." In this respect too Hale White is representative. The yearning for friendship and love, the hopelessness which ensues upon the frustration of this yearning, the "Stoical" resignation and dedication to a life of hard work, the bitter routine which ensues upon this hopelessness—this is the syndrome of his chief characters. For Arnold, to quote Mr. Trilling again, "the dominance of the rational intellect, the loss of the old intuitive knowledge is a sign of the aging and decay not merely of the individual but of the whole culture."[4] Arnold's own work shows his vacillation between the moral and the esthetic, between Hebraism and Hellenism. Hale White likewise is torn between the worship of authority and the delight in freedom: on one side of his life is the Father-oriented, rational religion of Calvinism, the strong man, the Carlylean hero; on the other side is the emotionally oriented religion of Wordsworth, the Romantic delight in beauty. His later novels indicate his development toward the esthetic and the free. Their shift from male to female protagonists is one sign of this. The subtle changes in the characters of the women themselves is another—from Miriam, who does not even consider breaking away from a husband she contemns, to Catharine, who has an affair with a married man, though she does not even consider having a sexual relation, to Madge, who does have such a relation. And then, as though this last breach were too much—as indeed Hale White's contemporaries considered it to be—Madge is overshadowed by the Pure Maiden, Clara, who triumphs through her denial of her instinctual life and, finally, through her denial of all her life, her martydom in the cause of Mazzini's Italy.

When the women do get closer to men than the lady of "A Mysterious Portrait," they never show a sign of carnality nor of sentimentality. From long training, Hale White's discipline holds him always in check from the crudely physical and the emotional. He is as well aware of the dangers of spirituality as of any other.[5] His control works wholly to his advantage, and it does so because it is completely natural to him. Even his restraint is concealed; it is never obvious understatement. And yet, displacing his quiet flow, there can sometimes be eloquence of Carlylean vigor, or flashing realism in the manner of Dickens.

The impact of these stories derives from their lifelikeness. Scene after scene has the quality of the unexpected, the naturalness of the accidental. They seem wholly uncontrived. There is never an intimation of a need on the part of the author to underscore or to manipulate. This quality may be the result of Hale White's approach to his fiction, which seems always a direct transcription, literal in its accuracy, from his own life. We remember that he said he never created a character but had always someone in his mind's eye as he wrote. The obverse side of this is that when he is compelled to manipulate the action, as he is in his novels in order to come to some conclusion, his hand becomes unsteady: sudden deaths, forced coincidences occur with a bewildering rapidity worthy of Hardy. Contrary to Hardy, however, "crass casualty" for him does not acquire philosophic dignity as a fictional equivalent to fate. For Hale White plot simply is not important. He frankly disregards its demands. It is beside his intent, which focuses on the character of exceptional people in most ordinary circumstances. These people are best revealed in almost disconnected scenes, fragments from the monotonous existence ordained for them. It is in this connection that the short stories come into their own. Sketches as they are, they can ignore the demands of plot. Because they are woven, as he said of one of them, "with a web of truth and a woof of fiction,"[6] they

## Themes of the Fiction: The Short Stories

allow Hale White's easy naturalness to follow its own course untrameled by any nineteenth-century canons about the "well made" plot.

"Mr. Whitaker's Retirement," to take an example, deals with a situation which bears interesting resemblances to Hale White's own. A man retires from a responsible position, in this case as senior partner of a large firm. Immediately his days become empty. A void stretches ahead of him. Then suddenly he loses all his money, and he is overjoyed. He goes back to work, to a life of happy routine as a humble clerk. When Hale White himself retired at the age of sixty after a long and successful career in the civil service (he was always proud of the letter from the Lords Commissioners expressing their warm appreciation of his services and "their regrets at parting with so valuable an officer") a void stretched out before him too, as his biographer notes.[7]

In contrast to Mr. Whitaker, the work upon which Hale White now embarked proved to be those writings, creative and critical, by which we now know him. Mr. Whitaker is in this respect a reflection of Hale White similar to Mark Rutherford, who likewise exhibits similarities to and interesting differences from his creator. (Mark thus after leaving college suffered the indignities of petty provincialism as a Dissenting and then a Unitarian minister, whereas Hale White, expelled from college, went on to London and an office job.) The differences are as significant as the similarities because they seem to project into Hale White's art the private struggles to which he allowed only this indirect expression, masked heavily, as we may recall, by a double veil of pseudonyms. The note of authenticity in these stories, as in the novels, comes from this combination of external verisimilitude and another kind of truth. Fiction, as Hale White uses it, has a way of emphasizing this other, poetic, truth. It may perhaps be this combination of essential truth with fiction which led William Dean Howells to say of Hale White's first two novels when they first appeared, in a phrase that may be excused for its exuberance, that "they marked a new era in fiction."[8]

CHAPTER 9

# *A Victorian Quest*

OUTSIDE of his fiction, Hale White's writing touched on a wide variety of subjects, ranging from astronomy to literary criticism. But he was not a dilettante. What makes his versatility so remarkable is his professionalism in those areas which interested him. Among his works are a translation from the Latin of Spinoza's *Ethic*, a treatise on politics, and a paper on sunspots read before the British Astronomical Association. These intellectual interests are, in fact, the same as those broached from various angles in his fiction. As a result, we shall have a chance to observe further how his works in fiction and in non-fiction illuminate one another. All his interests, moreover, have a common center which is basic to his novels: how to find a *modus vivendi* in a difficult world. This question and its answers constitute the substance of his religion, the key to his work and to his life. As such, his religion will be considered first in what may be called "the quest of a representative Victorian."

### I  *Varieties of Religion*

To the winds of doctrine in the nineteenth century, Hale White, versed as he was in the old dogma and in the new doubt, was finely sensitive. Religion as a sense of the cosmic was so natural to him that it colored not only his novels but all his thinking. "Now although many of us may more or less widely separate ourselves from the Christianity of the day," he observes, "Christianity is in our very blood and all our thoughts are coloured by it."[1]

Through the course of his life his concept of religion lived and grew with him, gradually changing into forms that would have been quite unrecognizable as religion to his forebears. Yet, just as he never lost his respect for authority in his search for new freedoms, so he never quite lost, in the eclecticism of his beliefs,

*A Victorian Quest*

the primary concept of religion as a revelation of the "truth"— that concept of mind underlying the universe which was the foundation of rational theology from Aquinas to Hegel. The youthful Mark Rutherford of the *Autobiography*, in attempting to answer the atheistic attack of Mardon, stated this basic position clearly: "It really seems to me of immense significance whether you see this intellect or not. . . . I believe that mind never worships anything but mind, and that you worship mind when you admire the level bars of cloud over the setting sun. You think you eject mind but you do not. I can only half imagine a belief that looks upon the world as a mindless blank, and if I could imagine it, it would be depressing in the last degree to me."[2]

Already his reinterpretation is beginning in the Wordsworthian reference to "the level bars of cloud over the setting sun." A childlike faith is impossible, Hale White notes in his journal; but "it is equally impossible to surrender it."[3] What he did was to reinterpret it. But the old, vital Calvinism was nonetheless in his "very blood," and this influence makes his religion such a motley coat and such a true reflection of the *sturm und drang* of the Victorian scene. "It is a mistake to suppose that the creed in which I had been brought up was or could be forever cast away like an old garment," he says in his *Early Life*. "The beliefs of childhood and youth cannot be thus dismissed. I know that in after years I found that in a way they revived under new forms, and that I sympathized more with the Calvinistic Independency of the sixteenth and seventeenth centuries than with the modern Christianity of church or chapel."[4] For this reason he drew the almost reverential portrait of that old Puritan, the Reverend Mr. Bradshaw in the *Revolution*, and contrasted it with a satiric one of that popularizer of a "modern" Christianity, the Reverend Mr. Broad. To those "new forms" in which the beliefs of his childhood were revived, his novels are devoted. They are shown in his protagonists' relations, esthetic and moral, to nature and to other people. The "ineluctable facts" of the old religion remain by whatever names, theological or psychological, we call them.

But under the stimulus of fresher currents of thought, religion acquired for him another layer of meaning. During his own long lifetime the Romantic reaction against rational theology developed into the agnosticism of the later Victorians. We have noticed the similarity between Hale White's *Autobiography* and Butler's *Way of All Flesh*, Mark Rutherford representing a halfway point on the road to that triumph of Victorian skepticism which culminates in Ernest Pontifex. The Romantic emphasis on experience, rather than on knowledge, as the essence of religion, directly influenced Hale White. In the world of his youth it was expressed in the many revivals of traditional faith—in English Evangelicism, in the Oxford Movement, in Continental Catholicism, in German Pietism. It was most clearly focused by the German theologians; and they, in turn, were echoed by Coleridge, by Carlyle (whose writings altered the religion of Hale White's father), by Matthew Arnold, and by the Broad Churchmen. The function of religion became esthetic and moral rather than intellectual, a way of living rather than a way of knowing. Arnold, for example, devoted a prodigious number of essays all through the 1870's[5] to the interrelated theses that religion is a matter of conduct, "an Eternal power not ourselves that makes for righteousness," that the truth of the Bible is the truth of experience, that the function of Christ was to teach us how to live. The *Broad Church Manifesto* of a decade earlier (1860) had attempted to show that the essence of Christianity lay not in its dogma or ritual but in its ethic and in the personality of Christ, together with a turning inward, a rebirth of the self. In their "Christian Socialism," Maurice and Kingsley combined religion with social service in what came to be called "muscular Christianity." All these themes are reflected in Hale White,[6] Christian Socialism being turned by him, for example, into the very substance of his *Deliverance*.

The fountainhead of this new criticism lay in Germany in the writings of its two brilliant theologians, Albrecht Ritschl and Friedrich Schleiermacher. Ritschl viewed religion as a form of action, or of behavior. It was, in Matthew Arnold's phrase, "Morality touched with emotion"; theology furnished symbols for moral ideals. Schleiermacher, reputed to have been "a great favorite" among some of Hale White's college professors,[7] was one of the first to formulate the concept of religion as symbolic and esthetic. For him the dogmas of religion became symbols of poetic insight. "Every finite thing is a sign of the Infinite."

"What is revelation? Every original and new communication of the Universe to man is a revelation. . . ."[8] Intuition is central. "Religion knows nothing of deduction and logical connections . . . everything is immediate and true for itself."[9] Issues of dogma are, for Schleiermacher, irrelevant to religion; truth or falsity is not its concern. Hale White's own experience at New College is echoed in Schleiermacher's words: "If you regard the systems in all schools, how often they are mere habitations and nurseries of the dead letter."[10] And, even as all Hale White's novels seek to relate the individual to the universe, so Schleiermacher sought "to understand an object as an element of the whole."

Put in its true context of the universal, even the most ordinary life assumes significance. When Baruch Cohen in *Clara Hopgood* identified the core of religion as the relationship of the individual to the whole, he added—as though it were a corollary—that religion was a "faith that the poorest and meanest of us is a person."[11] In their "uncovering of the commonplace," Hale White's novels present the ordinary under the aspect in which Schleiermacher says religion truly presents it: "The really religious view of things is to seek every trace of the divine, the true and the eternal, even in what seems to us common and base."[12] Professor John Herman Randall, Jr., has described Schleiermacher's religion as an esthetic experience with the whole universe as its object.[13] This is precisely the experience that the heroine of *Miriam's Schooling* has when she observes the stars and intuits the harmony of the cosmos; she is thus united with a universe beyond the boundary of her town of Cowfold. And, as a consequence, even Cowfold and her peasant-like husband assume dignity and meaning for her.

In his illuminating study of the genesis of modern concepts of the nature of religion, *The Role of Knowledge in Western Religion* (1958), Professor Randall has summarized the new view as one in which "the function of theology, or religious beliefs, of knowledge itself in the religious life [is] to serve as symbols not of concepts, not of knowledge, not of anything cognitive, but of feelings and attitudes or of values and commitments."[14] Hale White wrote his novels as documents in support of this view, just as William James, from another approach, wrote his *Varieties of Religious Experience*. For both men issues of dogma became irrelevant. Hale White always insists that the main question is: "How to live?" "Theology and metaphysics as *systems* must be failures," he says.[15]

For this reason Hale White regarded his study for the ministry as the great blunder of his life, "the mistake which well-nigh ruined it altogether."[16] "Ah yes," he writes to a friend, "I have often thanked God it is not my lot to be a professional teacher. ... It is surprising how much of what we, or at least I, hope, is based (I am talking of religion now) on what has no foundation which I can prove or exhibit. How then could I stand up and explain the way of salvation to people who must at all costs have simplicity and consistency?"[17] It is best to leave these intuitions in the nebulous state in which they come to us. "The demand for certainty is a sign of weakness, and if we persist in it, induces paralysis."[18] It is Pascal's "reasons of the heart" again, here supported by Romantic anti-intellectualism. This fideism Hale White derived ultimately from Wordsworth, who was the first, and the most profound, influence on his religious development. In a sense, he owes also to Wordsworth the initial motivation for his writing of fiction; for in his novels Hale White expressed the direction from authoritarian doctrine to individual experience of his Wordsworthian religion. He turned to the writing of fiction to express his discoveries much as an earlier Puritan would have turned to the writing of theology.[19]

Through the liberating effect of the *Lyrical Ballads*, the "artificial God of the churches" was replaced by a "living God." This statement is tantamount to saying that for Hale White the dead letter of belief was replaced by a living symbol. "If emotion be profound," he has remarked, "symbolism as a means of expression is indispensable."[20] Doctrines of belief become similitudes whose application each believer must find for himself. They are hence relative to the unique experience of each believer rather than irrevocably fixed for all. For this "heresy" Hale White had been expelled from New College. "But it was precisely this reaching after a meaning which constituted heresy," he says in the *Autobiography* concerning his attempt to interpret the creed in terms of "its natural origin in the necessities of human nature."[21] The atonement thus signified for him not so much an historical act as "a sublime summing up as it were of what sublime men have to do for their race." Hale White's is very much the same interpretation of religion as poetry which Santayana, who stood basically in the tradition of Schleiermacher, was in later years to make. It was also just such tracing of religious dogmas to their original sources in the needs of human experience which was advocated by Ludwig Feuerbach, whose *Essence of Christianity* George Eliot translated in 1854, during the period that Hale White was close to her. By his own probings, by his personal ties, and by the pervasive influence upon him of his milieu, Hale White was sufficiently motivated toward these new reinterpretations of religion.

Though his radical interpretations find their place in the larger context of Victorian thought, all Hale White's observations come to us as hard-won, intense personal insights to which the distinctive intimacy of his novels bears witness. As a way of living, religion becomes for him a form of esthetic experience. After he had been expelled from theological school, he was tossed into a battle for sheer existence in London. But his spiritual needs forced him to carve a bit of time out of each exacting day. And, as more leisure accrued to him after he had made a place for himself in life, fiction became the natural vehicle for his religious experience. His novels are the testament to his new discoveries in this realm.

## II  *The Political Dilemma*

Religion as a way of living rather than a way of knowing easily merged into programs for social amelioration. Religion thus became for nineteenth-century English socialists, whose thinking lay along moral rather than economic lines, a most useful institution. Social reform as a religious injunction was not very different indeed from the political egalitarianism of nonconformity itself. Hale White, close as he was to the contemporary "Christian Socialism" of Maurice and Kingsley, who (like William Booth, founder of the Salvation Army) combined religion with social service, makes the connection between religion and politics almost automatically.

Most of the Victorians regarded economic maladjustments not so much as social problems to be rationally solved but as moral evils to be deplored. After the manner of Carlyle and Ruskin, the correction they envisaged was to come mainly as a moral revolution from within. Hale White follows this line. He quotes approvingly, for example, Wordsworth's belief "that the world is running mad with the notion that all evils can be relieved by political changes, political remedies, political nostrums—whereas the great evils, sin, bondage, misery lie deep in the heart, and nothing but virtue and religion can remove them." Hale White's own approach, to which his *Deliverance* bears eloquent witness, is to deplore. "It was an awful thought to me," he says in it about the London slums, "ever present on those Sundays and haunting me at other times, that men, women and children were living in such brutish degradation, and that as they died others would take their place. Our civilization seemed nothing but a thin film or crust lying over a volcanic pit, and I often wondered whether some day the pit would not break up through it and destroy us all."[22] In the *Revolution in Tanner's Lane* the hero's political activities were the natural extension of his religious enthusiasm. In words that ring with passion, Hale White in this novel voices the never quite suppressed fury of the poor against the rich. Zachariah is shown there hunting for a job, only to be met by contempt and insolence:

Talk about the atrocities of the Revolution! All the atrocities of the democracy heaped together ever since the world began would not equal, if we had any gauge by which to measure them, the atrocities perpetrated in a week upon the poor, simply because they are poor; and the marvel rather is, not that there is every now a September massacre at which all the world shrieks, but that such horrors are so infrequent. Again, I say, let no man judge communist or anarchist till he has asked for leave to work, and a "Damn your eyes!" has rung in his ears.[23]

In this passage the moral indignation of Cromwellian nonconformity, for which religion became essentially a social protest, may be observed. Nonconformity had the history pratically of an underground movement; its members were a repressed minority who even in Hale White's youth could not, to take one example, be admitted to Oxford or to Cambridge. Revolution was in Hale White's blood mixed with his Puritanism. His grandfather had been a Radical, the windows of whose house had been smashed by a Tory mob (the one-year old Hale having to be snatched quickly out of his cradle in the front room) because he refused to illuminate for the English their victories over the

## A Victorian Quest

French—a scene which Hale White used to open his *Revolution in Tanner's Lane.*

The question of the locus of political power, whether it should be divided atomistically among all the members of society or centralized in the state, was troubling the minds of men in the nineteenth century almost as much as it was to do in our time. John Stuart Mill wrote the classical liberal defense of individual freedom in his *On Liberty*. The authoritarian view, apart from Carlyle's thunderous advocacy, was more subtly, and more ambiguously, conveyed in Matthew Arnold's *Culture and Anarchy*. Arnold's was a concept of leadership by men of "culture." Culture for him resembled religion in its study of perfection, but went beyond it in its "harmonious expansion of *all* the powers which make the beauty and worth of human nature." (Arnold's concept is only vaguely authoritarian, since the ideal leadership for him becomes a composite of the "best self" of every man; it resembles Hale White's view of the natural aristocrat drawn from the ranks of the common man.) Hale White reflects both the liberal and the authoritarian approaches in combinations that at times seem paradoxical. (The same can be said of Puritanism, with its equally strong theocratic and democratic tendencies.) He defends universal suffrage in true liberal vein. A stronger vein in him, however, is basically opposed to rule by the majority. His ideal of government, which he nowhere fully outlines, seems to be one embodied in a great man whose actions spring from noble principles, a fundamentally religious man.

When Hale White took a page from history, in his *Revolution*, it was a sorry tale of inefficient leadership and swift retribution on the part of the powers-that-be against the abortive uprisings in Manchester. Socialism, whose philosophy had seeped into his attitudes, he did not see as workable. "Socialism towards which everything is drifting may turn out a great failure," he remarks. "In my opinion it will certainly fail, and the reaction will be disastrous and put us back beyond where we are now; but at any rate socialism is an *idea*, and in so far as it aspires to govern the world by an idea, it is progress."[24] In contrast to this ambivalence regarding socialism, his ideal of religious leadership is clear-cut; it accommodates itself almost too easily to the cult of the hero. It is adumbrated in his fictional portraits of strong men, like Mr. Bradshaw, in the *Revolution*. Such a man he saw in Mazzini, whom he portrayed in his last novel and whom he visited in London. "I spent one evening almost alone with Mazzini," he records in a letter. "He was living then under a feigned name in very humble lodgings in Brompton. He had much of the saint in him, and consequently it was difficult, for me at least, completely to sympathize with him. Imperfection of sympathy, however, did not prevent admiration, almost enthusiastic, for him, especially for his sublime courage and for his faith in certain Ideals to which he gave the name of God. In his purity and simplicity of worship he was altogether un-English, admitting no compromises, a true believer in the celestial kingdom and the New Testament."[25] When Hale White has Clara and Madge Hopgood visit Mazzini in London, as he himself had done, Mazzini is made to expound a theory of government in which an appeal must be made "to something above the people."[26]

Hale White's own suggestions for reform were embodied in a pamphlet called an *Argument for an Extension of the Franchise* (1866). It may seem paradoxical in the light of his pessimism concerning rule by the majority that Hale White's own work of a strictly political nature should be a pamphlet advocating an extension of the franchise. But, turning from his vision of an ideal leader to the facts which pressed around him, one can understand why he shelved his vision in favor of feasible proposals. His own town supplied an amplitude of such facts: "Hastings is an old-fashioned, corrupt, jobbing, rotten borough, and its municipal government is a joke."[27] Obviously, something drastic had to be done. But the initial goals would have to be attainable within the given political context. The franchise was, especially after Chartist agitation, a recognized area for reform. Nor should it be forgotten that Hale White's nonconformist background would lead him not only to a respect for great men as leaders but also to a rejection of entrenched privilege. Furthermore, the ambivalences of his Romantic heritage were at work in him too: the exaltation of both the exceptional genius and the common man. In a sensibility as responsive as his to the crosscurrents of attitudes in his age, democracy and aristocracy did not exclude each other. In his novels they are, in fact, made to merge into each other; the common man is discovered to be a natural aristocrat.

In relying exclusively on a political remedy, Hale White

*A Victorian Quest*

shows the Chartists' bias and limitations. The Chartists of the 1840's concentrated chiefly on just this measure of extending the base of government through the franchise. In common with them, as well as with English socialists generally, Hale White emphasizes the need for individual freedom. He does not attack the economic cause of social rot—the inhuman, calculating, selfish code of political economy—as did, for example, Carlyle, Dickens, and Ruskin.

### III  *Consolation of Philosophy*

Hale White was driven, it might seem against his will, up the long road of speculative thought. He could, he writes his son, "no more escape from the urge towards philosophical enquiry than a bird can help flying."[28] He devoted many hours of his life to Spinoza, translated him from the Latin in a work that became a standard text of the *Ethic*. At the very start, we are met by an apparent contradiction between his urge toward philosophy and his anti-intellectualism. He is severest on just those tendencies which he senses to be strong within him. Especially severe is he on abstract systems of thought. He scents the danger of unreality in the imposition of an arbitrary framework upon a fluid composition of events. To get at things as they are, thinking must grow quite literally out of passion or, in other words, out of the self immersed in the process of living. "If there be such a thing as passionless thinking," he makes one of his characters say, "it does not lead to much. Emotion makes intellectual discoveries."[29] Systems of thought become more unreal as they become more consistent: "The contact of a *system* of philosophy or religion with reality is that of a tangent with a circle. It touches the circle at one point, but instantly the circle edges away."[30]

This objection is the one that the Romantics brought against eighteenth-century rationalism. When thinking sacrifices consistency, then it may become useful. Its use is ethical. This concept is as true for Hale White in philosophy as it was for him in religion. Speculation is justified to the extent that it gives help. So, although he opposes metaphysical elaboration, he does so in the ultimate interests of philosophy, exactly as he opposed theology in the interests of what he conceived to be true religion. Philosophy retains its hold ethically, which means *relevantly* to human needs: "If a man holds sincerely to any theory of life it is better than none. Any system which gives unity and subordinates motives is an advantage."[31] His emphasis is that of Romantic philosophy on the integration of all the being or soul of man. Philosophy then becomes an articulation of the complete range of experience and, like religion, partakes of the nature of poetry or "myth." Keats spoke in one of his letters of proving the axioms of philosophy on his pulses. This explains the meaning of Hale White's "anti-intellectualism." It is an "existential" opposition to the kind of philosophy which, to borrow some more of Keats's words, "will clip an Angel's wings,/Conquer all mysteries by rule and line,/Empty the haunted air. . . ." It is opposed to "gray theory" ("*Grau ist alle theorie*," Goethe had said); it is for the participation of the whole person in the processes of existence. What we believe is not of so much importance, Hale White more than once says, as the path by which we travel to it.

Hale White discovered to his delight a unifying philosophy in Spinoza: "I have . . . found his works productive beyond those of almost any man I know of that *acquiescentia mentis* which enables us to live."[32] This kind of help was what Hale White most needed, as his *Deliverance* shows: an ability, call it stoical or Spinozistic, to resign himself and so gain peace of mind in the face of monotony and drudgery. In all his painstaking analysis of Spinoza's dialectic, what sustains him is the moral insight that is so potent because it is so pervasive and beautifully implicit. Spinoza is a prophet who leads rather than thunders. He teaches gently, without histrionics. His effect is, in the rhetorically saturated age in which Hale White lived, like that of a modernized *Imitation of Christ* or of *Pilgrim's Progress*, to which works Hale White compares Spinoza's.[33] Spinoza supplied him with a solution to his problems in terms which satisfied his intellectual standards and which yet did not conflict with his religious and poetic instincts. "What a region is this into which we are here introduced," he says in his preface to the *Ethic* concerning Spinoza's propositions on God: "there is no writer probably who loosens more effectually the hard tyranny of time and circumstance and provides us with more of those thoughts which it is the office of a real and speculative religion to supply." Spinoza's appeal to the nineteenth-century mind, with its need for a unifying concept of God and the universe, a concept that would satisfy its Romantic assumption that experience comes

## A Victorian Quest

nearer to truth than rational thought, is evident—aside from the parallels between Spinoza's and Wordsworth's thought—in such representative Victorians as George Eliot (who translated Spinoza's *Ethic* at about the same time as did Hale White) and Matthew Arnold. (In his book on Arnold, Lionel Trilling has demonstrated Arnold's dependence on Spinoza, Arnold's close identification of his own aims and methods with those of Spinoza, and the part played by Spinoza's *Tractatus Theologico-Politicus* in Arnold's concept of religion).[34]

By Spinoza, Hale White was helped first of all to his emancipation from the intellectual doubts of his age, those doubts which had battered Mark Rutherford and Zachariah Coleman. In all his novels the development of Hale White's heroes is a process of release from the human bondage which Spinoza identified. This release, in Hale White's terms, is from enslavement to petty relationships and routines through initiation to the universal in man and nature. Zachariah, for example, could relate his trial with that of Christian in *Pilgrim's Progress* and so "he could give it a place in the dispensation of things, and could therefore lift himself above it."

For Hale White, Spinoza also gave religion a new place in the new world; and, by so doing, Spinoza helped to save men from the demons of doubt, or from the unpleasant alternative of materialism: "It was he who relieved men, or who did his best to relieve them, from the trouble and despair consequent upon what is really a dual government of the world, and it was he who gave vitality and practical meaning to the great doctrine of the unity of God. Lastly, he may be said to have contributed something towards a truly human religion."[35] Hale White had to face within himself a difficult problem centering on the ingrained dualism of Western tradition, in its separation of matter and spirit and in its even sharper division between good and evil. Moreover, he never surmounted this problem. The Christian, and more particularly Puritan, dichotomies between right and wrong, spirit and flesh, "higher" and "lower" faculties in man were all soundly unified by Spinoza. This unification had a magnetic appeal to Hale White, but he could not completely possess it himself. Even the phrase in the quotation above, "what is really a dual government of the world," shows that he was himself divided.

During the years Hale White was rewriting his long preface to the *Ethic*, in reality an essay which involved "a re-reading of [Spinoza] through from end to end" (as he remarks in a letter), he was also at work on his last novel, *Clara Hopgood*. There, in his tender portrait of Baruch Cohen, he projected his love for Spinoza. Baruch, who bears Spinoza's Hebrew name, leads the sheltered life of a speculative thinker who devotes himself to the delightfully impersonal pursuit of the One in the Many. "I believe," he is made to say, "that all thought is a manifestation of the Being, the One, whom you may call God if you like...."[36] In Baruch, Hale White has created an idealized image of the true philosopher. The gentleness of Baruch's nature mirrors Baruch's inner unity and this characteristic draws Clara Hopgood to him and gives their relationship its distinctive quality, a love which is like a religious experience. (So it had been for the original philosopher in the Christian heritage, Plato, who taught that love is a passion for unity, for wholeness.) In his beneficent influence on Clara, Baruch quite literally illustrates how Spinoza "gave vitality and practical meaning to the great doctrine of the unity of God."

Spinoza's approach toward a central unity was prompted by his own need to reconcile the old religion and the new mathematical science of his day. Instead of allowing science to displace religion, to obliterate the traditional concepts of soul and spirit, as the raw materialism, the "atomism," of the later seventeenth century threatened to do,[37] Spinoza combined the concepts of body and mind, of a mechanically deterministic universe and an omnipresent God. He actually identified them. The way that Spinoza did this for Hale White resulted in an illumination that remained with him throughout his long life: "A saying of Spinoza, which I first read fifty years ago, has remained with me ever since," he tells us, and gives the quotation: " 'The mind and the body are one and the same individual which at one time is considered under the attribute of thought, and at another under that of extension" (Prop. XX1, pt. 2, Schol.). God became for Spinoza immanent in the universe (as he had been for the Stoic philosophers, whom Hale White admired) rather than exalted above the universe like the transcendent Father in Heaven. Both God and the universe were in this way brought within the compass of human understanding. Both were, so to speak, "human-

# A Victorian Quest

ized." This "humanization" is, of course, what also happened to Wordsworth's God and Universe, resulting in their similar power over Hale White's imagination and "converting" him to his own poetic version of religion.

Not only did Spinoza support those religious attitudes which had early been shaped by Wordsworth, but he appealed to the dominant moral vein in Hale White. Ethical meaning is in fact, Hale White stresses, the *raison d'être* of Spinoza's metaphysics. Spinoza's concern with knowledge lay in the fruit it could bear through its cultivation in living. "The ontology is subsidiary," as Hale White puts it. Spinoza's ontology is relevant only as it helps us to reach our maximum capability, helps us to the "third kind of knowledge," from which springs the supreme good, "the intellectual love of God." Spinoza's ontology, then, is imbued with ethical purpose. By means of his metaphysical system alone, we come to know and love God, and so to achieve the highest happiness and the ultimate end of living. Knowledge *is* virtue: "the effort to understand," Spinoza says, "is the primary and sole foundation of virtue."[38] Spinoza's chief work, that in which he expounds his ontology, he therefore called not a *Metaphysic* but an *Ethic*.

Spinoza offered Hale White, as he offered Matthew Arnold, a solution which organized all phases of human activity, emotional and intellectual. Of this solution it truly could be said that "it gives unity and subordinates motives." In his preface to the fourth and last edition of the *Ethic*, Hale White gives practically his final word on the subject: "I also desire again to remind the reader that Spinoza's aim was ethical, or search, as he says, for that 'by whose discovery and acquisition I might be put in possession of a joy continuous and supreme to all eternity'; for those 'clear and distinct ideas' through which 'a passion ceases to be a passion.'"[39]

## IV  Science and Ethics

"The thoughts which have worked upon me, and perhaps have changed me, have not been those which men usually consider the most important," Hale White remarks in the first sentence of an essay called "Revolution."[40] The title refers to the revolution worked out within himself. The three influences that he chooses as pivotal for him are Spinoza, astronomy, and Wordsworth. The delights of astronomy he discovered late in life. But, as with his response to Wordsworth and Spinoza, the basis had been laid early. The sky was always that part of the natural scene which especially excited his imagination—its morning tints, its daytime cloud formations, its night-long displays. It afforded a direct line to the "universal" which for him was a necessity. Once Hale White started astronomical observations, they supported the routine of his days to the very end. That the orientation was already there with the young man is indicated in the *Autobiography*. After his initial, depressing service as Unitarian minister, Mark Rutherford was walking home in the rain, lonely and miserable. "But just before I reached home," he records, "the clouds rolled off with the south-west wind into detached, fleecy masses, separated by liquid blue gulfs, in which were sowed the stars, and the effect upon me was what that sight, thank God, always has been—a sense of the infinite, extinguishing all mean cares."[41] At the age of eighty he got up at four in the morning in order to see a comet. His letters and journals are studded with astronomical observations such as the following one, made in 1911: "I saw Mars and Saturn last night. I have also, wonderful to relate, seen Mercury for two mornings running by walking to the top of our hill between six and seven. Very few people have ever seen him, he is always so near the sun."[42]

The role that astronomy played in his life may be gauged from a sentence in the *Revolution in Tanner's Lane*: "We all have too vast a conception of the duty which Providence has imposed upon us; and one great service which modern geology and astronomy have rendered is the abatement of the fever by which earnest people are often consumed."[43] Astronomy provided a rationale in modern terms for the insights which had been first awakened in him by the poetry of Wordsworth and later articulated by the philosophy of Spinoza. In so doing, it fulfilled the ethical function which Spinoza attributed to knowledge: it freed Hale White; it helped him to understand, or, as Spinoza put it, to love God. Hale White's progress in this direction under the therapeutic influence of his science is reflected especially in *Miriam's Schooling*, in which astronomy provides the tutelage for Miriam's emancipation. Through it she learns to enlarge her limited experience, to transcend the confines of a provincial town and a dull marriage. As she begins to comprehend the heavens, her esthetic perceptions are sharpened; she responds to their beauty, which hitherto, like most people, she has ignored. She responds also to her husband's scientific mind and then to her husband himself. Astronomy thus serves for her a function analogous to that of religious conversion; it develops her awareness of her relation to the universe, helps her to feel unified within herself and with the world.

In describing Miriam's initiation, Hale White's words achieve a cogency which seems to issue directly from his own experience: "In the profounder study of the science, there is perhaps no pleasure so sweet and so awful as that which arises, not when books are read about it, but when the heavens are first actually watched, when the movement of the Bear is first actually seen for ourselves, and with the morning Arcturus is discerned punctually over the eastern horizon; when the advance of the stars westwards through the year, marking the path of the earth in its orbit, is noted, and the moon's path also becomes intelligible."[44] It is in the Reverend Mr. Armstrong, however, that the pervasively moral influence of astronomy appears. The study had a "strange fascination" for him. He never preached or wrote about it; it was locked up inside him. Yet, ironically enough for this minister of the Gospel, "It was for some inexplicable reason the food and medicine which his mind needed. It kept him in health, it pacified him, and contented him with his lot."[45] It served him truly as a religious function. When "a good way past middle life," Hale White himself became the possessor of a telescope. "Almost every clear night I spent hours in simply *looking*, with never failing wonder," he records. "When I went into the observatory on a winter's night, when I shut the door, opened the roof, and set the driving-clock going, the world and its cares were forgotten. How could they be remembered in the presence of Perseus, awful, beautiful, without hurry, rest, acceleration or delay. . . ." Astronomy in fostering that serenity which is the condition of the good life, "pacified" the Reverend Mr. Armstrong. Contemplation, which arouses the instinct for beauty, emancipated Miriam. The pursuit of the stars is inseparable from the enjoyment of the universe.

In spite of his moral emphasis, the impression that astronomy meant to Hale White little more than a psychological release or a convenient approach to the study of human nature would be inaccurate. As in all his interests, the moral implications certainly are significant. But they are not insisted upon. Miriam, for example, gains her happiness not by philosophizing on the relation between herself and the universe, but by forgetting her problems and finding a gratuitous pleasure in her orrery and in the configurations of the stars. This empirical approach the Reverend Mr. Armstrong is made to impress upon Miriam and her husband before they are even allowed to look into his telescope: "If you can once from your own observation realise the way the stars revolve—why some near the pole never set—why some rise, and why Venus is seen both before the sun and after it—you will have done yourselves more real good than if you were to dream for years and years of immeasurable distances, and what is beyond and beyond, and all that nonsense."[46]

Hale White's own special investigation focused on the physical constitution of the sun. In her diary, Mrs. White gives us some notes made by a young visitor to Hale White, and these afford a glimpse of Hale White at work. There are drawings of "'daily observations for days after days,'" very neat drawings "'of the spots on the sun as seen through a spectroscope.'"[47] In a letter of June, 1894, during the period he was gathering material for his paper on sunspots, Hale White discloses his patient search into the sun's constitution: "As for stars, I don't know, but they may have gone out altogether. I have been waiting to catch one particular star for three weeks, but in vain. One day, however, we had some pure sunshine, and as I had a spectroscope lent me, I managed to see for the first time in my life what are called 'prominences' that is to say, the solar eruptions, enormous masses of ruddy hydrogen flame shooting some seventy or eighty thousand miles above the sun's edge. I shall never forget that spectacle."[48]

The paper, "The Wilsonian Theory of Sunspots," which he was at this time preparing, and which later, on January 30, 1895, he read before the British Astronomical Association, is a model of careful research because Hale White had a respect for literal accuracy, an attitude encouraged perhaps by his long years of political reporting. This attitude also accounts for the attention to minute detail of scene and personality in his novels, which imparts to them their distinctive impression of literal, living truth. Like Tennyson, Hale White is always meticulous about the accuracy of his details. He would never allow himself that latitude of which he finds abundant evidence in other literary men: "The list of blunders made by literary people when they describe the sky at night," he remarks in an article on Tolstoy's astronomy, "would be a long one, and they do but reflect the general ignorance."[49] If this approach made Hale White's fiction so convincing, it also allowed him to achieve the professional touch in his science.

## V  *The Literary Sensibility*

Hale White is also chary of speculative judgments. His literary comments bear the imprint of his scientific self-education: "There would be no objection to 'telling the truth' about Burns, Byron and Shelley if it could be told. But it cannot be told. We are informed that they did this or that, and the thing they did is to us what it would be if done by ourselves."[50] About the correctness of text, for example, he is fastidious, and once this is assured, he allows himself few flights. "I think it ought to be the object of lecturers and essayists, talking about a great man," he observes, "to stimulate people to read him, to show them in his own words what he is, and not use him as an opportunity for displaying themselves. For my own part, I have seldom found brilliant critical essays of much use to me. I always look for the inverted commas."[51] Reflected here is his trust in experience again, and his anti-intellectualism. He himself has a remarkable gift for quotation.

Hale White's literary sensibility is, of course, implicit in both the authors he chooses—and those he neglects. He is most concerned with nineteenth-century poets. Those outside the century have a "romantic" appeal—Shakespeare, Milton, Spenser. The great non-Romantic poets like Chaucer, Donne, Dryden, and Pope are rarely mentioned. Although Byron is one of Hale White's heroes, he does not refer to his satiric poems. Quite unconsciously, moreover, Hale White adopts definite critical positions that naturally derive from his basic attitudes. He is "anti-literary" because facing life is for him primary. Literature has a utilitarian, or moral, function—to give help. For this reason Shakespeare, Wordsworth, Johnson, Bunyan and the Bible appeal to him. "Poetry, if it is to be good for anything, must help us to live," he says. "It is to this we come at last in our criticism, and if it does not help us to live it may as well disappear, no matter what its fine qualities may be."[52] This view he imbibed early from Carlyle, who had in 1850 written the young Hale, eighteen at the time, "to *practise* what you learn" in his books; Carlyle had then added: "It is idle work otherwise to write books or to read them."[53]

Hale White acquired also a Carlylean delight in physical élan, the kind of sanative vitality he finds, for example, in Byron (whom he characterizes as "a mass of white hot coal"). Like a true Romantic, Hale White trusts impulse rather than reason. "The wave does not hesitate to break upon the shore, but hurls itself headlong in magnificent blindness," says one of his characters, in an attack on "the life of the cultivated class."[54] Hazlitt had vaunted "gusto" in art as the "power or passion defining any object." Matthew Arnold had said that genius is energy. All Hale White's fiction is a celebration of energy, whether it be manifested in the flaming sincerity of his early heroes or in the moments of heady "enthusiasm" in all of them. Mark Rutherford in the *Autobiography* was drawn to people who, like himself, had had "an enthusiastic stage in their history." For Hale White such enthusiasm itself leads to wholeness, as well as to that spiritual nobility which Arnold found best exemplified in Homer and other Classics.

In one of his essays, "The Morality of Byron's Poetry," Hale White says, "We do not understand how moral it is to yield unreservedly to enthusiasm, to the impression which great objects would fain make upon us, and to embody that impression in worthy language."[55] Enthusiasm offers for him a gateway to the universal. It leads to an alliance with those "great objects" which offer release from the petty, introspective ego. The voluminousness and vitality of Sir Walter Scott he loves for the same reason. "Scott demands," he says in connection with *The Monastery*, "not so much critical penetration, as a capacity for rejoicing, for emotion, a shut door against indifference, a heart full of hope and enthusiasm." It is by instilling this temper that Scott has justified his popularity among people bound to a gray existence.[56]

Hale White's literary criticism reaffirms the bias of his religion and philosophy, which countered the artifices of creeds and systems with the freshness of immediate experience. Of Charlotte Brontë, for example, he says that she, like Byron, "is imperish-

## A Victorian Quest

able because she speaks under overwhelming pressure, self-annihilated, we may say, while the spirit breathes through her." The artist is the voice of nature. His power is that of the elemental universe itself; his strength therefore is "sanative." It is opposed to the sickly introspection and the affectation of "literary" and "cultivated" people.[57] There is a kind of primitivism implicit here. Enthusiasm is for Hale White salutary, freeing the self to expand to its truly heroic dimensions. In words that ring like Carlyle's, Hale White proclaims, "Strength is true morality and true beauty."

For all his love of the "commonplace," Hale White shares the Victorian penchant for the grand style. In fact his "uncovering of the commonplace" means for him a revelation of the heroic hidden in it. All the heroes of his stories display the soaring spirit of the man "elevated" by God, the natural aristocrat extolled by Emerson and Carlyle. For Zachariah Coleman, Byron articulates the ache of existence: "The lofty style, the scorn of what is mean and base, the courage—root of all virtue—that dares and evermore dares in the very last extremity, the love of the illimitable, of freedom." These qualities point Zachariah toward his own final freedom. The moral and aristocratic poet sounded the nobility that lay within the poor little printer of Rosoman Street, Clerkenwell. Zachariah is in this respect a reflection of Hale White's own father, also a printer, and one of those thousands in the early decades of the century who used to repeat Byron's verse "by the page."[58]

The concept of the "heroic style" is itself in its origin related to an uncovering of the commonplace, stemming as it does in part from the revival of folk literature—of Homer conceived as a strolling bard of the people, and of the old English ballads. The features of the heroic or grand style were moral. These Ruskin had isolated in *Modern Painters*; his chapter, "Touching the 'Grand Style,'" had stressed that it is the product of "men in a state of enthusiasm," of "men who feel *strongly* and *nobly*." Such men were precisely Hale White's ideal in both his creative and his critical writing. Matthew Arnold had perhaps succeeded best in defining the ineffable qualities that Hale White sought to embody in his own fiction and to discover in his authors: "The grand style—but what *is* the grand style?" Arnold, who had asked this question in his lecture *On Translating Homer*, had answered that it arises "when a noble nature, poetically gifted, treats with simplicity or with severity a serious subject."

The kind of ideal that Hale White seeks in literature is his personal version of Puritan salvation in a world lost to Puritan theology. His is close—again—to Arnold's persuasion that literature may assume the role of a lost faith in helping us to relate the results of modern science to our need for conduct, our need for beauty. Hale White's concept is close to the Romantic conception of poetry as essential truth, "the breath and finer spirit of all knowledge," in Wordsworth's phrase; "the center and circumference of knowledge," in Shelley's. Hale White's view verges likewise on the Romantic construct of the "genius," whom, as frequently, Carlyle describes in a form closest to Hale White's sense. In *Heroes and Hero Worship*, the literary writer becomes a latter-day prophet; "The true literary man," Carlyle says, is "the light of the world, the world's priest;—guiding it, like a sacred Pillar of Fire, in its dark pilgrimage through the Waste of Time." Literature can save us by uniting us, as Hale White says Byron and Charlotte Brontë do, to the strength of the universe itself. Literature for Hale White is judged—as his politics, his philosophy, and his science were—in the existential terms of his new religion.

## CHAPTER 10

## *Achievements*

IN a little sketch called "The Preacher and the Sea," Hale White depicts a man, against the backdrop of the vast ocean, bellowing at a huddled handful of people. "Believe in the Lord. You are all wounds and bruises and putrefying sores," he shouts at them. They are going fast to a place "where shall be wailing and gnashing of teeth for ever and ever." The sketch ends with these words: "Sunny clouds lay in the blue above him, and at his feet summer waves were breaking peacefully on the shore, the sound of their soft, musical splashing filling up his pauses and commenting on his texts."[1] Nature's ironic comment betokens the new Wordsworthian religion.

The ardor of the old Puritan religion, emasculated of its theology, is focused by Hale White on human problems. Men and women have "great, gaping needs" which must somehow be satisfied. A question that is of our time as well as of his becomes the *leitmotif* of all his writing: how to live in a confused and often alien world; how to achieve at least the sense of balance; and beyond that, the sense of unity with all that is, which, from both a theological and a psychological point of view, is the *summum bonum* of religion. Hale White's phrasing of the question is often theological, in terms of his old, inherited religion; but his meanings move steadily in the direction of modern pragmatism and, in a broad sense, of "existentialism." For this reason all the facets of his writing—fiction, philosophy, politics, science, and literary criticism—react so continuously on one another and reflect his new religion. They all emphasize "engagement." For his protagonists, this engagement can culminate at the best in a sense of unity.

Two significant twentieth-century writers on religion define this engagement by those aspects which Hale White discovered in his own life and developed in his fiction. The first formal principle of theology, says Paul Tillich, is an "ultimate concern," which "is the object of total surrender, demanding also the surrender of our subjectivity while we look at it."[2] This precisely expresses what happens to such two different characters in Hale White's novels as the young, unschooled Miriam Tacchi and the elderly, learned Baruch Cohen: the former is possessed by the starry universe; the latter, by the One. The word "concern," Tillich notes, "points to the 'existential' character of religious experience." In *A Common Faith,* John Dewey describes religious faith as a "unification of the self through allegiance to inclusive ideal ends, which imagination presents to us and to which the human will responds as worthy of controlling our desires and choices."[3] Hale White's various protagonists owe allegiance to various ideal ends, imaginatively conceived in love, science, philosophy, and politics. Ordinary people that they are to start with, their progress, like that of Bunyan's Christian, is impeded, often faltering. Their progress is toward unification, and it constitutes the pervasive theme of his fiction. His working out of this theme is his "uncovering of the commonplace," which can, in the great moments of his stories, lead to a revelation of the "order of splendor" (the happy phrase by which John Herman Randall, Jr., distinguishes the religious dimension in human experience).[4] These are the contexts, then, departing widely from those of the old orthodoxy, in which Hale White may be termed a "religious" writer. Like so many of the thoughtful Victorians, he speaks cogently and humanely to the concerns of his time and of ours; and his doing so makes him representative of his age.

Within the ample range of Victorian fiction, moreover, Hale White has made one area particularly his own. In the small world of provincial nonconformity he has depicted the exaltation and heroism, as well as the degeneration and hypocrisy, of human beings caught in a time of change. For these people, who were his own, he became the principal voice in the nineteenth-century novel. His tones reverberate with a passionate seriousness, but they are always controlled, often lightened, by the play of a dry wit.

The basis of Hale White's appeal is the honesty of his work. In his novels the brusque, incalculable flux of experience is given immediately. Plots do not count, scenes do. These features

*Achievements*

—together with the "biographical" approach, the representation of the story as a chronicle of life, without suspense, without a sign of artifice—are part of the credo of the Naturalistic novel, with its illusion of unedited life, as it was to be developed toward the end of the century by such practitioners as Zola, Gissing, and Moore. Hale White is a forerunner in the Naturalistic tradition, although he combines with it elements of lyric feeling and moral intensity, as well as of spiritual disclosure, which are often absent in the full-blown "Naturalistic" novel. His prose style itself is natural in the best sense; it is as uncontrived as his narrative. It is a medium clear and plain, an index of his own taste, and an anticipation of the "functional" mode of the twentieth century, from the prose of Hemingway to the buildings of Frank Lloyd Wright.

There is one injunction which we may imagine Hale White followed in all his work: " 'My boy,' my father once said to me, 'if you write anything you consider particularly fine, strike it out.' "[5] This austerity of diction corresponds with his spareness of narrative. His emotional scenes are almost never played up, but owe their effect to a sense of proportion which seizes only the essential features of the situation. Their power lies in the sense they convey of passion under check, of human complexities beyond the reach of words. He writes in the vein of the best Puritan authors of the past. The influence of the Bible's simple style and narrative economy is evident throughout. For such qualities as these Hale White's fellow authors admired his work. The tributes of William Dean Howells and Edmund Gosse have already been noted in the Preface. To these can be added the report of how Matthew Arnold "enthused" over Mark Rutherford.[6] In similar strain, Arnold Bennett called *The Revolution in Tanner's Lane* "the finest example of modern English prose,"[7] and André Gide in his journals expounded upon the basic honesty of Hale White's work. "Here honesty and integrity," wrote Gide, "become poetic virtues beside which everything seems camouflaged, unauthentic, and overloaded. . . . The very style of William Hale White (Mark Rutherford) is exquisitely transparent, scintillatingly pure. He develops to perfection qualities that I wish were mine. His art is made of the renunciation of all false wishes."[8]

Hale White is, in short, interesting intrinsically and historically. An unusually keen sensibility, he illustrates in how many ways, subtly and unexpectedly, the personality of the artist can enter his art. An unusually attuned spirit, he serves as a dependable barometer for the Victorian climate of opinion. From his frank self-revelations, we gain a strangely intimate insight into the moral environment of the nineteenth century. In its variety and sureness of taste, his work can be regarded as a minor monument of the Victorian period.

In every age certain minor figures—poets, philosophers, divines, men of sensibility—reflect with accuracy and charm the convictions and doubts, the unconscious assumptions, and the biases and tastes of their contemporaries. They may do this with even more cogency than do the giants of the day, whose genius has a way of transmuting current patterns. One thinks of Joseph Glanvill and Henry More in the seventeenth century, of Shaftesbury and Chesterfield in the eighteenth century, of Dorothy Wordsworth and that recently discovered diarist, Francis Kilvert, in the last century. Such a key figure for his own time is William Hale White.

# Notes and References

### Preface

1. William Dean Howells, "Editor's Study," *Harper's New Monthly Magazine*, LXXII (February, 1886), 485.
2. Edmund Gosse wrote this in a review of Hale White's *Pages from a Journal* and *More Pages from a Journal*, in the *Morning Post* (London, November 14, 1910). Quoted by Irvin Stock, *William Hale White (Mark Rutherford), A Critical Study* (New York, 1956), p. 3.
3. The references by these authors to Hale White are to be found in the following sources: Aldous Huxley, ed. *The Letters of D. H. Lawrence* (New York, 1932), p. 83; Arnold Bennett in the *New Statesman*, XXII (October 13, 1923), Supplement, p. viii; G. Jean-Aubry, ed., *Joseph Conrad: Life and Letters* (London, 1927), I, 335; John Berryman, *Stephen Crane* (New York, 1950), p. 248; *The Journals of André Gide*, trans. Justin O'Brian, 4 vols. (New York, 1947-51), II, 101; III, 337-38.
4. Catherine Macdonald Maclean, *Mark Rutherford, a Biography of William Hale White* (London, 1955); Stock, *William Hale White*; Wilfred Stone, *Religion and Art of William Hale White ("Mark Rutherford")* (Stanford, 1954).

### Chapter One

1. *Groombridge Diary*, p. 195.
2. *Autobiography*, p. 19.
3. *Last Pages*, p. 289.
4. *Ibid.*, p. 278.
5. *Groombridge Diary*, pp. 471-72.
6. *Last Pages*, p. 289.
7. *Ibid.*, p. 308.
8. *More Pages*, p. 210.
9. *Autobiography*, p. 98.
10. *Early Life*, p. 80.
11. *Groombridge Diary*, p. 75. See *Letters*, p. 274.
12. *Ibid.*, pp. 479, 475.
13. *Autobiography*, p. 98.
14. *Letters*, p. 289.
15. *Groombridge Diary*, p. 23.
16. *Letters*, p. 331.
17. *Groombridge Diary*, p. 73.

18. *Ibid.*, p. 36.
19. Emile Legouis and Louis Cazamian, *A History of English Literature* (New York, 1926), II, 430-31.
20. *Groombridge Diary*, p. 33.
21. *Ibid.*, p. 176.
22. *Ibid.*, p. 36.
23. *Early Life*, pp. 83-85; *More Pages*, p. 120.
24. *Groombridge Diary*, p. 182.
25. *Deliverance*, p. 97.
26. *Groombridge Diary*, p. 121.
27. *More Pages*, p. 225.
28. *Ibid.*, p. 65.
29. *Groombridge Diary*, p. 28.
30. *More Pages*, pp. 195, 187. Cf. *More Pages*, pp. 149-50, 243; *Last Pages*, pp. 314-17.
31. Of Morris he gives an amusing account in a letter: "Morris, Earthly Paradise Morris came to dinner with us. He is unlike any fancy picture which the imagination might draw of him. He is broad-shouldered, ruddy, wears a blue shirt with no necktie, and talks with great vehemence; oftentimes with a kind of put-on roughness I think —as if he meant to say, 'If you think that I am an Earthly-Paradisiacal creature with wings, you are egregiously mistaken.'" *Letters*, p. 155. See also pp. 6, 52-53, 82, 245; *Autobiography*, p. xii.
32. *Letters*, p. 245.
33. George Jackson, "Mark Rutherford's Scrap Books," *London Quarterly Review*, CXXXI (April, 1919), 200.
34. *Letters*, p. 301. Cf. pp. 30, 388; *Groombridge Diary*, pp. 29, 77. For other painters or paintings he names, see *Letters*, pp. 121, 193, 338; *Groombridge Diary*, p. 104.
35. *Letters*, pp. 175, 180. Cf. p. 382.
36. *Ibid.*, p. 290. Cf. pp. 382, 371, 387; *Groombridge Diary*, p. 396.
37. *Ibid.*, pp. 378, 296. Cf. pp. 258, 393.
38. *Groombridge Diary*, p. 375. William Robertson Nicoll, *Memories of Mark Rutherford* (London, 1924), pp. 29-30. Cf. *Letters*, p. 387; *Groombridge Diary*, p. 19; *Autobiography*, p. 125.
39. *Groombridge Diary*, p. 340.
40. William White, *The Inner Life of the House of Commons*, ed. Justin McCarthy, 2nd ed. (London, 1898), p. xxii.
41. "Traffic," *Crown of Wild Olive*.
42. *Letters*, p. 161. On the Victorian "moral aesthetic" see Jerome H. Buckley, *The Victorian Temper* (Cambridge, 1951), Chapter VIII.
43. *Catharine Furze*, p. 131. Cf. pp. 277-78.
44. *Pages*, pp. 290-91.
45. *Autobiography*, p. 8.

## Notes and References

46. *Ibid.*, p. 61.
47. *Ibid.*, p. x.
48. *More Pages*, p. 153.
49. W. Hale White, *John Bunyan* (New York, 1904), pp. 221-22.
50. *Letters*, p. 213.
51. *Ibid.*, p. 311.
52. *Groombridge Diary*, p. 9.
53. *The Athenaeum*, No. 3031 (November 28, 1885), 702.
54. *More Pages*, p. 3. From a letter by Carlyle dated March 9, 1850.
55. *Ibid.*, p. 233. See *Last Pages*, p. 119.
56. *Clara Hopgood*, p. 237.
57. *Miriam's Schooling*, p. 110.
58. *Groombridge Diary*, p. 56.
59. *Athenaeum*, LXXVII (April 23, 1881), 555.
60. "Editor's Study," pp. 485-86.
61. *Catharine Furze*, pp. 8-9; *Early Life*, p. 32. On Constable see C. R. Leslie, *Memoirs of the Life of John Constable* (London, 1911), pp. 1-2.
62. *Groombridge Diary*, p. 66.
63. See C. Silvester Horner, *Nonconformity in the XIXth Century* (London, 1907), p. 89 for the conformist viewpoint of Dickens' contribution to our understanding of nonconformity; *Groombridge Diary*, p. 198.
64. W. L. Sperry, "Mark Rutherford," *Harvard Theological Review*, VII (April, 1914), 173.
65. *Autobiography*, p. 26.
66. *Revolution*, pp. 123-24.
67. *Groombridge Diary*, p. 66.
68. *Catharine Furze*, p. 302.
69. *Pages*, p. 107.
70. *Last Pages*, pp. 289-90.
71. *Autobiography*, p. 20.
72. *Pages*, p. 8.
73. W. J. Dawson, *The Makers of English Fiction* (New York, 1905), places *The Autobiography of Mark Rutherford* in a class he calls the "religious novel." This he defines as "that which centers itself expressly, definitely, and by distinct limitation on the exposition of religious ideas or the statement of theological problems. It may take into its scheme a wide or narrow area of human action, but it will take no more than is necessary to its special purpose. It may create types of character as vital as any that may be found in more secular forms of fiction, but that is a question of the power of the artist, not the intention of his art. In other words, the religious novel is a novel in

which the faculty of creative imagination is definitely devoted, and in some instances subordinated, to the exposition of religious ideas." Even within this somewhat lenient definition it is, however, difficult to accommodate the *Autobiography* (not to mention Hale White's later novels), which certainly does not center itself on "the exposition of religious ideas or the statement of theological problems." It centers itself on the hero, Mark Rutherford; theological problems are only passing incidents, however searing, in Mark's development. Beside the *Autobiography* Dawson finds only a few other novels that fit into his classification. He names *David Elginbrood* and *Robert Falconer* by George Macdonald, *John Inglesant* by J. H. Shorthouse, *Robert Elsmere* by Mrs. Humphrey Ward, and *The Story of an African Farm* by Olive Schreiner. A more recent study of the religious novel of the Victorian age, Margaret Maison, *Search Your Soul, Eustace* (London, 1961), points out the distinctive position achieved by Hale White's novels because of their sincerity, depth, and restraint. She singles out Hale White's *Autobiography* and Mrs. Humphrey Ward's *Robert Elsmere* as the "two Victorian religious novels that have survived the acid test of time and remain as classics in the literature of lost faith."

74. *Autobiography*, p. 32. Cf. Dawson, p. 270.

75. An interesting side light on his methods of attaining this directness occurs in his advice to a friend: "Don't bother yourself with corrections, don't write with anybody before your eyes, don't use an important looking manuscript book, but rather odd envelopes or at best odd half sheets." *Letters*, p. 261.

76. T. Seccombe, "The Literary Work of Mark Rutherford," *Living Age*, CCLXXVII (May, 1913), 498-99.

77. *Last Pages*, pp. 244-45, 247.

## Chapter Two

1. *Letters*, p. 11; *Groombridge Diary*, p. 124.
2. *Autobiography*, pp. 109-110.
3. Maclean, p. 262.
4. *Early Life*, p. 5.
5. *Letters*, p. 281.
6. *Early Life*, p. 51.
7. It was this political liberalism and its attendant publicity that caused both the failure of William White's business in Bedford and the start of his successful career in London. In Bedford the clerical customers dropped away from his bookstore because of his liberal views. Lord John Russell, the prominent Whig who had in the course of the battles between Whigs and Tories come to know White and to recognize his merits, got him the appointment to the House. It was

## Notes and References

through the connections that White made there that Hale was later to get his first appointment to his career as a civil servant. William White also preceded his son in writing letters for the provincial journals on the activities in the House. These were later collected and published as *The Inner Life of the House of Commons*.

8. *Early Life*, p. 39.
9. *Ibid.*, p. 72.
10. *Ibid.*, p. 74.
11. Quoted by Maclean, p. 226.
12. *Early Life*, pp. 30, 38.
13. *Autobiography*, p. 4.
14. *Ibid.*, pp. 5, 6.
15. *Early Life*, p. 45. Cf. *Autobiography*, p. 8.
16. *Letters*, p. 65.
17. *Early Life*, p. 57.
18. Though there is a similarity in subject between Hale White's *Autobiography* and Gosse's book, their approach is quite different. This difference has been well put by W. L. Sperry: "Unlike Gosse, Mark Rutherford tells the story with humility and pain and deep feeling for the tragic transition through which he is passing. He could never be satisfied with Gosse's facile iconoclasm. To him the renunciation of old creeds and the casting off of outworn systems is a painful self-mutilation." Sperry, "Mark Rutherford," p. 183.
19. *Early Life*, p. 59. Cf. *Autobiography*, pp. 9-11.
20. *Ibid.*, p. 55.
21. *Ibid.*, pp. 61-63. Compare Mill's account of Wordsworth's influence on him: "What made Wordsworth's poems a medicine for any state of mind, was that they expressed, not mere outward beauty, but states of feeling, and of thought coloured by feeling under the excitement of beauty."
22. *Autobiography*, p. 18.
23. Cf. *Early Life*, pp. 38, 62.
24. *Early Life*, pp. 62-63.
25. *Autobiography*, pp. 13, 21.
26. *Early Life*, p. 79 ff.; *Groombridge Diary*, p. 463; W. R. Nicoll, *A Bookman's Letters* (New York, 1913), p. 371. For an account of Hale White's expulsion from New College I am indebted to *Early Life*, p. 63 ff. and to Stone, p. 32 ff. The quotations from the Principal's Inaugural Lecture are taken from the latter book.
27. *Sartor Resartus*, Book II, Chapter 7.
28. *Autobiography*, pp. 36-37.
29. See Walter E. Houghton, *The Victorian Frame of Mind, 1830-1870* (New Haven, 1957), p. 228 ff., for a discussion of this distinction.

30. *Autobiography*, p. 29.
31. *Ibid.*, p. 54.
32. *Ibid.*, p. 57.
33. The explanations of the existential "absurd" by its exponents read like modern versions of the Victorian plight of Mark Rutherford in the *Autobiography*. Albert Camus puts it this way: "A world that can be explained by reasoning, however faulty, is a familiar world. But in a universe that is suddenly deprived of illusions and of light, man feels a stranger. His is an irremediable exile, because he is deprived of memories of a lost homeland as much as he lacks the hope of a promised land to come. This divorce between man and his life, the actor and his setting, truly constitutes the feeling of Absurdity." And Eugene Ionesco says this: "Absurd is that which is devoid of purpose. . . . Cut off from his religious, metaphysical, and transcendental roots, man is lost; all his actions become senseless, absurd, useless."
34. *Autobiography*, p. 93.
35. *Early Life*, p. 80.
36. *Ibid.*, p. 82; *Autobiography*, pp. 125-26. The letter by Hale to his father is quoted by Maclean, p. 118.
37. *The Athenaeum*, No. 3502 (December 8, 1894), 790.
38. *Last Pages*, p. 132.
39. *Autobiography*, p. 127.
40. *Ibid.*, p. 131.
41. *Groombridge Diary*, p. 72. The sympathy between these two, the personal relationship between whom it was "a lasting sorrow" to Hale White that he allowed to languish, was to emerge in their common concern with Spinoza (both translated his *Ethic* at about the same time, in the 1850's), and in the closeness of subject matter and theme of the novels they were later to write. George Eliot's first work of fiction, *Scenes of Clerical Life*, as well as *Adam Bede* and *Mill on the Floss*, all are concerned with a milieu and type of character not unlike Hale White's own. Both start with religion as personal and central; both are concerned with its growth and transformation; both celebrate the heroism of ordinary people. Both also re-create the scenes of their early lives, George Eliot's *Scenes of Clerical Life* doing for the provincial Anglicanism of her native Warwickshire what Hale White's novels do for the provincial Dissent of his Bedfordshire.
42. *Autobiography*, p. 134.
43. Dawson, *The Makers of English Fiction*, p. 286.
44. *Groombridge Diary*, p. 51.
45. *Early Life*, p. 30.
46. *Ibid.*, p. 31.
47. *Autobiography*, p. 50.

*Notes and References*

48. Lady Robert Cecil, "Mark Rutherford," *The Nation and Athenaeum*, XXXIV (October 27, 1923), 151; *Early Life*, p. 31.
49. Sperry, "Mark Rutherford," p. 175.
50. *Autobiography*, pp. 94, 103.

*Chapter Three*

1. About five years after his marriage in 1856, his wife developed disseminated sclerosis, a creeping paralysis of the nervous system, which attacked first her legs, then her arms, then her eyes. It killed her finally in 1891. Housekeepers had to be kept, so that in addition to all the unhappiness, his privacy was destroyed. To this misfortune Hale White's critics have been tempted to trace the recurrent theme of marital incompatibility in Hale White's fiction, in view especially of the autobiographical nature of his stories. The testimony of his children and all Hale White's own references to his wife indicate only their complete devotion to each other.
2. Quoted by Stock, pp. 76-78.
3. *Deliverance*, p. 159.
4. In his notebooks Hale White more than once returns to such Stoical admonitions. Cf. "We must not worry ourselves with attempts at reconciliation. We must be satisfied with a hint here or there, with a ray of sunshine at our feet, and we must do what we can to make the best of what we possess." *Pages*, p. 75; Cf. *Pages*, pp. 64, 119.
5. *Autobiography*, pp. 114-15.
6. *Deliverance*, p. 1; *Early Life*, p. 33. Nicoll, *A Bookman's Letters*, p. 387.
7. *Deliverance*, pp. 23, 18, 64-65.
8. *Ibid.*, p. 28.
9. *Ibid.*, p. 27.
10. Maclean, p. 154.
11. Quoted by D. G. Somervell, *English Thought in the Nineteenth Century* (London, 1954), p. 112.
12. We know that at least one of the books Hale White liked to read to his assembled family at tea-time on Sundays was Kingsley's *Heroes*. The leading idea of Christian Socialism was incorporated also in one of the most popular novels of the period, Mrs. Humphrey Ward's *Robert Elsmere* (published in 1888, three years after the *Deliverance*). Robert Elsmere's development parallels Mark Rutherford's—from orthodox minister to skeptic to social worker. Elsmere, having given up his clerical calling, migrates to London and founds in its slums a humanitarian project which avoids specific religious affiliation, calling itself the "New Brotherhood"; it emphasizes the "essentials" of Christianity, its ethical and human aspect. Unlike Hale

White's novels, *Robert Elsmere* is "literary" and technically clever in a manner Hale White would have disdained. It was such a resounding success that it was shamelessly pirated, a factor leading to the passage of the International Copyright Bill of 1891.

13. In his book on Ruskin, Professor John Rosenberg has indicated clearly the Christian background of British Socialism in connection with Ruskin's own development: "Only a fraction of those who became Socialists were converted to the movement by Marx. As Clement Atlee wrote, the party was built up largely by ardent Christians: "In no other Socialist movement has Christian thought had such a powerful leavening effect. . . . British Socialism, unlike its counterparts on the continent, has always been essentially Ruskinian—rather than Marxist and doctrinaire. Far more than we realize, the economic revolution of the twentieth century is the culmination of the religious revival of the nineteenth. For that revolution represents not simply the triumph of the modern, secular ideal of equality, but also a striving toward the ancient religious one according to which, in Ruskin's words, "Christ's gift of bread, and bequest of peace, shall be 'Unto this last as unto thee.'" "Atlee points out," Mr. Rosenberg adds, "that even today one is more likely to hear Scripture quoted on the platform of the Socialists than on those of all other parties." John Rosenberg, *The Darkening Glass, A Portrait of Ruskin's Genius* (New York, 1961), pp. 143-44.

14. *Early Life*, pp. 74-77.
15. Cited by Stone, p. 139.
16. *Deliverance*, p. 25.
17. *Ibid.*, p. 65.
18. *Ibid.*, p. 113.
19. *Ibid.*, pp. 32-33.
20. Miss Leroy is modeled upon a childhood favorite of Hale White: "I had an aunt in Colchester, a woman of singular originality, which none of her neighbors could interpret, and consequently they misliked it, and ventured upon distant insinuations against her. . . . In summer-time she not infrequently walked at five o'clock in the morning to a pretty church about a mile and a half away and read George Herbert on the porch. . . . The survival in my memory of her cakes, gingerbread, and kisses, has done me more good, moral good . . . than sermons or punishment." *Early Life*, pp. 11-12.
21. *Groombridge Diary*, p. 2.
22. *Ibid.*, pp. 264-65.
23. *Deliverance*, p. 106.
24. *Ibid.*, p. 103.
25. *Autobiography*, p. 19.
26. *Deliverance*, p. 107.

## Notes and References

27. In his disparagement of the intellect as a result of painful soul searching, Mark resembles a later rebel against the religious tradition, Ernest Pontifex in Butler's *Way of All Flesh*. The careers of Mark Rutherford and Ernest Pontifex are remarkably similar. Both are brought up in a narrow faith and become ministers of religion. Both are victims of the unscrupulous and hypocritical orthodox. Both doubt the literal truth of the Bible and both become anti-intellectual in reaction against rational theology. Butler goes further than Hale White, however, in his rejection of Christianity. Whereas Hale White reinterprets it in secular terms, Butler rejects it altogether as fraudulent and harmful, a hoax on the part of the older generation. Ernest's release from orthodoxy leads him to Darwinism as an article of faith and to the cynical enjoyment of the "luxury of a quiet, unobtrusive life of self-indulgence." Mark Rutherford represents a half way point on the way to the ultimate triumph of Victorian skepticism over dogmatism. Ernest Pontifex represents its culmination. I am indebted to Maison, *Search Your Soul, Eustace*, pp. 278-83, for her discussion of *The Way of All Flesh*.
28. *Deliverance*, pp. 127-28.
29. *Letters*, p. 157.

### Chapter Four

1. *Pages*, p. 147.
2. *Ibid.*, p. 130.
3. *Revolution*, pp. 135-36.
4. *Last Pages*, p. 225.
5. *The Bookman*, II (August, 1892), 140.
6. *Revolution*, pp. 183-84. Carlyle, *Past and Present*, Book III, Chapter 15.
7. *Revolution*, pp. 36-37.
8. *Ibid.*, p. 24.
9. *Ibid.*, p. 90.
10. *Ibid.*, pp. 105, 137-38.
11. *Ibid.*, p. 10.
12. *Ibid.*, p. 327; Nicoll, *Memories of Mark Rutherford*, p. 34.
13. *Revolution*, p. 67.
14. *Ibid.*, p. 74.
15. *Ibid.*, pp. 89, 75, 77, 92, 213.
16. *Ibid.*, pp. 215, 146.
17. *Ibid.*, p. 69.
18. *Ibid.*, pp. 18-19.
19. *Ibid.*, p. 253.
20. Nicoll, *A Bookman's Letters*, pp. 368-69.
21. *Revolution*, p. 279.

22. *Ibid.*, pp. 252, 290-91.
23. *Ibid.*, p. 336.
24. *Ibid.*, p. 343.
25. *Ibid.*, p. 95.
26. *Ibid.*, p. 100.

## Chapter Five

1. *Miriam's Schooling*, pp. 64-65.
2. Stone, p. 147; Maclean, p. 332.
3. *Groombridge Diary*, pp. 48-49.
4. *Miriam's Schooling*, pp. 52, 58, 114, 121, 141.
5. *Ibid.*, pp. 100-1, 132.
6. *Ibid.*, pp. 55-57, 62.
7. *Ibid.*, pp. 68, 81-82, 113.
8. *Autobiography*, p. 19.
9. Quoted from unpublished letters by Stone, p. 148.
10. *Miriam's Schooling*, pp. 118-19.
11. *Autobiography*, p. 18.
12. *Miriam's Schooling*, pp. 77, 78.
13. Maclean, p. 38; cf. *Letters*, p. 249.
14. *Miriam's Schooling*, p. 137.
15. *Ibid.*, p. 146.
16. *Ibid.*, pp. 147-48.
17. *Early Life*, pp. 23-26.
18. *Miriam's Schooling*, pp. 97-98.

## Chapter Six

1. *Catharine Furze*, pp. 24-25.
2. *Ibid.*, p. 239.
3. *Ibid.*, pp. 73-74. Hale White's letter on contemporary houses appeared in Ruskin's *Fors Clavigera*, Letter 75, for March, 1887. The house that Hale White finally built for himself was solid, devoid of stucco and the wedding-cake gothic that both he and Ruskin, who came to consult with him as it was a-building, loathed. Maclean, pp. 177-78. Cf. *Letters*, p. 329.
4. *Catharine Furze*, p. 72. Hale White's dislike of modern innovations in old churches is evident in his letters, in such passages as the following one on a church in the East Quantocks: "Inside the church is beautiful wood carving *and*—close to the canopied tomb, under the shadow of the fifteenth- and sixteenth-century architecture, with the purple hills on the horizon, the parson has stuck the gaudiest of altars with maroon cotton velvet curtains, ordered probably from the cata-

## Notes and References

logue of the ecclesiastical furnishers and tailors in Southampton Street. So much for the converting power of beauty! But I do believe that no religion from that of Ashtoreth to that of Mormon has ever had a *sillier* and obtuser priesthood than ours." *Letters*, pp. 184-85.

5. *Catharine Furze*, pp. 189, 192.
6. *Ibid.*, pp. 109-10.
7. *Ibid.*, pp. 148-70.
8. *Ibid.*, pp. 188-89.
9. *Ibid.*, p. 192.
10. *Ibid.*, p. 114.
11. *Ibid.*, pp. 104, 125.
12. Cardew's relation with Catharine in this respect curiously anticipates the relation that Hale White himself was to enjoy with Dorothy Vernon Smith. There is an uncanny similarity between the way Cardew's little story, "Did He Believe?" prefigured his relation with Catharine and the way this novel itself prefigures Hale White's own essential relation with Dorothy Vernon Smith. It is as though Hale White were here preparing himself for the great, climactic experience of his last years, when in 1907, fourteen years after the publication of *Catharine Furze*, he was, at the age of seventy-seven, to meet Miss Smith, and three and a half years later to marry her.
13. *Catharine Furze*, pp. 212, 213-14.
14. Hale White in extolling the eloquence of Caleb Morris, says, "I shall never forget a sermon of his on the prodigal son. He dwelt not so much on the son as on the father. . . . He pointed out that this parable, although it taught us the depth of God's love, was a glorification by Jesus of human love. I can feel even now the force that streamed from him that night, and swept me with it, as if I were a leaf on a river in flood." (*Last Pages*, p. 245.) Mr. Cardew's sermon on the same subject has the same effect on Catharine. It seems probable that Hale White is here recapturing a vivid scene from his own life.
15. *Catharine Furze*, pp. 217-18, 222-23.
16. Compare Emerson's phrase in "The Oversoul": "Jove nods to Jove from behind each of us."
17. *Catharine Furze*, p. 162.
18. *Ibid.*, pp. 332-33.
19. *Ibid.*, p. 342.
20. *Ibid.*, p. 365.

### Chapter Seven

1. *Clara Hopgood*, p. 8.
2. *Autobiography*, p. 17.
3. *Clara Hopgood*, pp. 29-30.

4. *Ibid.*, p. 39.

5. *Ibid.*, pp. 85-89. Review of *The Poetical Works of William Wordsworth* (edited by William Knight, Vol. VIII, Macmillan and Co.), *The Athenaeum*, No. 3648 (September 25, 1897), 412.

6. *Clara Hopgood*, p. 157.

7. *Ibid.*, p. 99.

8. *Ibid.*, p. 162. In his *Doctrine and Discipline of Divorce*, Milton castigated the Canon Law for preposterously making "careful provision against the impediment of carnall performance" and ignoring the much more serious impediment of an "unconversing inability of minde."

9. Claudius Clear (W. R. Nicoll), "Mark Rutherford," *British Weekly*, XX (July 9, 1896), 185.

10. "Clara Hopgood," *The Nation (London)*, LXIII (September 3, 1896), 180.

11. *Letters*, p. 164.

12. *Clara Hopgood*, p. 181.

13. *Deliverance*, pp. 109-10.

14. *Clara Hopgood*, p. 275.

15. *Ibid.*, pp. 245-46.

16. George Eliot was intimately associated with his translation of Spinoza's *Ethic*; she also made a translation of the same work during the days they knew each other. Clara resembles George Eliot in her independence and unconventionality. She also resembles George Eliot physically, especially in the luminosity of her gray eyes; of Clara, Hale White observes, "Her eyes were gray, with a curious peculiarity in them . . . occasionally . . . they ceased to be mere optical instruments and became instruments of expression, transmissive of radiance to such a degree that the light which was reflected from them seemed insufficient to account for it." In his notebooks he said of George Eliot: "in her gray eyes there was a curiously shifting light, generally soft and tender, but convertible into the keenest flash." (*Clara Hopgood*, p. 5; *Last Pages*, p. 132.) Clara Hopgood seems thus to be associated by Hale White with two of his idols, Spinoza and George Eliot.

17. *Clara Hopgood*, p. 182.

18. *Ibid.*, p. 223.

19. *Ibid.*, p. 234.

20. *Ibid.*, p. 171.

21. *Ibid.*, pp. 33-34.

22. *Ibid.*, p. 265.

23. *Ibid.*, pp. 283-85. Cf. *Miriam's Schooling*, pp. 151-53.

24. *Clara Hopgood*, pp. 292-93.

25. *Ibid.*, pp. 269-71. In the *Aberdeen Herald* for December 12,

*Notes and References*

1868, he wrote of Mazzini's stirring talk: "When I first saw him, many years ago, that was what chiefly struck me. Before I had been with him more than a few minutes he was driving at something which filled him with interest—it was some philosophical question if I recollect—and we were discussing it as if we were the oldest of friends, and had been with one another all day long . . . no man was ever loved more, and none that I ever saw realized more perfectly in faith and private life the ideal of a Christian saint." The quotation from the *Aberdeen Herald* is taken from Maclean, p. 331. Cf. *Letters*, p. 193.

26. *Clara Hopgood*, p. 44.

27. Hale White had in his youth known just such a girl as Clara, one who became devoted to the cause of Italian freedom when she met Garibaldi on his visit to England. Hale White admired her nobility and her quiet strength. (Maclean, p. 99). George Levine in "*The Cocktail Party and Clara Hopgood*" compares Hale White's with T. S. Eliot's handling of the problem of salvation: the way of martyrdom and the way of acceptance of ordinary life. Hale White, he argues, "makes the alertness seem real while Eliot does not." *The Graduate Student of English*, I (Winter, 1958), 5-6.

28. Arnold Bennett, *The Journal of Arnold Bennett* (New York, 1933), III, 28.

## Chapter Eight

1. *Miriam's Schooling*, p. 155.
2. *Ibid.*, pp. 156-57.
3. *Deliverance*, p. 170.
4. Lionel Trilling, "Matthew Arnold," *Major British Writers*, (New York, 1954), II, 426-27.
5. *Last Pages*, p. 68. Cf. *Deliverance*, p. 95.
6. *Groombridge Diary*, p. 181.
7. Maclean, pp. 270-71.
8. "Editor's Study," pp. 485-86. This may be compared with one of the latest judgments on Hale White, by Margaret Maison, in her study of the religious novel in the Victorian age (published in 1961): "Intensely personal, completely sincere, and devastatingly sombre, the *Autobiography*, as a confession of doubt, stands supreme in English fiction." Maison, *Search Your Soul, Eustace*, p. 255.

## Chapter Nine

1. *Letters*, p. 146.
2. *Autobiography*, p. 84.
3. *Pages*, p. 86.

4. *Early Life*, p. 78; Cf. *Revolution*, p. 127. Compare this observation which his second wife records in her *Groombridge Diary*: "This was the world in which I lived, not the world of clever critics, or of literature, or of art for its own sake, nor yet the world of professedly dogmatic teachers, but a religious world." *Groombridge Diary*, p. 15.

5. *St. Paul and Protestantism*, 1870; *Literature and Dogma*, 1873; *God and the Bible*, 1875; *Last Essays on Church and Religion*, 1877.

6. Margaret Maison, in *Search Your Soul, Eustace*, shows how popular novels of the day capitalized on these new religious trends in a way Hale White himself did not, by exploiting, sensationally or sentimentally, religion as art, as in J. H. Shorthouse's *John Inglesant* (1880); religion as social service, as in George Macdonald's *David Elginbrood* (1863) and *Robert Falconer* (1868); and the personality of Christ and other New Testament figures, as in Disraeli's *Tancred* (1847), Lew Wallace's *Ben Hur* (1880) and most of the fashionable novels of Marie Corelli.

7. Maclean, p. 75.

8. Friedrich Schleiermacher, *On Religion, Speeches to its Cultivated Despisers* (New York, 1958), pp. 88-89.

9. Quoted by R. B. Brandt, *Philosophy of Schleiermacher* (New York, 1941), p. 115.

10. Schleiermacher, p. 16.

11. *Clara Hopgood*, p. 276. Maclean, p. 218.

12. Quoted by Brandt, p. 97.

13. J. H. Randall, Jr., *The Role of Knowledge in Western Religion* (Boston, 1958), p. 86.

14. *Ibid.*

15. *Last Pages*, pp. 269-70. All Hale White's religious convictions echo the following words of Carlyle in *Heroes and Hero Worship*: "By religion I do not mean here the church creed which he professes, the articles of faith which he will sign . . . But the thing a man does pratically believe . . . concerning his vital relations to this mysterious universe and his duty and destiny—there! . . . That is his *religion*, or it may be his mere skepticism and *non-religion*."

16. *Early Life*, p. 55.

17. *Letters*, p. 176.

18. "Principles," *Deliverance*, p. 165.

19. Matthew Arnold's thinking also took this direction as is illustrated in his famous statement that "most of what now passes with us for religion and philosophy will be replaced by poetry."

20. *More Pages*, p. 225.

21. *Autobiography*, p. 21.

## Notes and References

22. *Deliverance*, p. 65. Wordsworth quoted by Hale White in *An Examination of the Charge of Apostasy Against Wordsworth* (London, 1898), p. 16.
23. *Revolution*, p. 135.
24. *Last Pages*, p. 254.
25. *Letters*, p. 193.
26. *Clara Hopgood*, pp. 270-71.
27. *Letters*, p. 72. Cf. *Letters*, pp. 69-70.
28. Quoted from private notes by John Harry White, Hale White's second son, in Stone, p. 71.
29. *More Pages*, p. 74.
30. *Ibid.*, p. 240. Cf. *Last Pages*, pp. 129-30, 269-70.
31. *Last Pages*, p. 266.
32. *Pages*, p. 58.
33. *Ibid.*, p. 32.
34. "Preface" to the *Ethic* . . . by Benedict de Spinoza, translated from the Latin by W. Hale White; translation revised and corrected by Amelia Hutchinson Stirling, 4th ed. (London, 1910), pp. XXV, XXVI. For Arnold's references to Spinoza see Lionel Trilling, *Matthew Arnold* (New York, 1924), esp. pp. 272, 324-27, 329-31.
35. Preface to Spinoza's *Ethic*, pp. XCIII-XCIV.
36. *Letters*, p. 61; *Clara Hopgood*, p. 277.
37. Hale White conceived materialism in the older terms of a mechanistic universe, as Spinoza did, rather than in the newer terms of evolution. Hale White's problem of the opposition between science and theology, oriented as it was toward older concepts, was thus especially amenable to such solutions as Spinoza proposed.
38. Spinoza's *Ethic*, pp. 200, 274, 275. Cf. *Ethic*, Part IV, Prop. XXVIII: "The highest good of the mind is the knowledge of God, and the highest virtue of the mind is to know God."
39. Preface to Spinoza's *Ethic*, p. 274.
40. *Last Pages*, p. 88.
41. *Autobiography*, p. 95.
42. *Letters*, pp. 131, 387. Cf. *Letters*, pp. 65-66, 88, 327, 366.
43. *Revolution*, pp. 355-56.
44. *Miriam's Schooling*, pp. 143-44.
45. *Ibid.*, p. 140.
46. *Ibid.*, pp. 140-41.
47. *Groombridge Diary*, p. 226.
48. *Letters*, pp. 65-66.
49. "Tolstoy's Astronomy," *The Athenaeum*, No. 3870 (December 28, 1901), 879. Letter.
50. *More Pages*, p. 225.
51. *Pages*, p. 213.

52. *Ibid.*, p. 108.
53. *Ibid.*, p. 3.
54. *Ibid.*, p. 343.
55. *Ibid.*, p. 130.
56. *Revolution*, pp. 276-77.
57. *Pages*, pp. 147-48.
58. *Revolution*, p. 25; *Early Life*, p. 37.

## Chapter Ten

1. *More Pages*, pp. 157-58.
2. Paul Tillich, *Systematic Theology* (Chicago, 1951), I, 12.
3. John Dewey, *A Common Faith* (New Haven, 1934), p. 33.
4. Randall, *The Role of Knowledge*, p. 120 ff.
5. *Early Life*, p. 31.
6. Matthew Arnold is reported, at second hand, to have always "enthused" over Mark Rutherford. He told a friend "on no account ever to miss anything that Mark Rutherford ever wrote." Quoted from an unpublished letter in Stock, p. 3, n. 2.
7. Arnold Bennett, in the *New Statesman*, XXII (October 13, 1923), Supplement, p. VIII.
8. *The Journals of André Gide*, III, 338.

# Selected Bibliography

### PRIMARY SOURCES

Only the published works of Hale White are listed here. For a more complete bibliography, including a full listing of unpublished material and periodical writing, see the Bibliography in Wilfred Stone, *Religion and Art of William Hale White* ("Mark Rutherford"). See also Simon Nowell-Smith's *Mark Rutherford: A Short Bibliography of the First Editions.* Supplement to *The Bookman's Journal*, 1930.

1. Original Works

*An Argument for an Extension of the Franchise.* London: F. Farrah, 1866.
*A Letter Written on the Death of Mrs. Elizabeth Street.* London: W. P. Griffith & Son, 1877. Privately printed and circulated.
*The Autobiography of Mark Rutherford, Dissenting Minister.* Edited by His Friend, Reuben Shapcott. London: Trübner & Co., 1881.
*A Dream of Two Dimensions.* Printed for private circulation, 1884.
*Hymns, Psalms & Anthems.* Compiled for George's Chapel, Exeter. Exeter: *Devon Weekly Times Office*, 1884. Hymn 119.
*Mark Rutherford's Deliverance, Being the Second Part of His Autobiography.* Edited by His Friend, Reuben Shapcott. London: Trübner & Co., 1885.
*The Revolution in Tanner's Lane.* By Mark Rutherford. Edited by His Friend, Reuben Shapcott. London: Trübner & Co., 1887.
*The Autobiography of Mark Rutherford and Mark Rutherford's Deliverance.* Edited by His Friend, Reuben Shapcott. 2d ed: Corrected and with Additions. London: Trübner & Co., 1888.
*Miriam's Schooling and Other Papers.* By Mark Rutherford. Edited by His Friend, Reuben Shapcott. London: Kegan Paul, Trench, Trübner & Co., Ltd., 1890.
*Catharine Furze.* By Mark Rutherford. Edited by His Friend, Reuben Shapcott. 2 vols. London: T. Fisher Unwin, 1893.
*Clara Hopgood.* By Mark Rutherford. Edited by His Friend, Reuben Shapcott. London: T. Fisher Unwin, 1896.
*An Examination of the Charge of Apostasy Against Wordsworth.* London: Longmans, Green & Co., 1898.
*Pages from a Journal With Other Papers.* By Mark Rutherford. London: T. Fisher Unwin, 1900.
*John Bunyan.* London: Hodder and Stoughton, 1904.
*More Pages from a Journal With Other Papers.* By Mark Rutherford. London: Henry Frowde, Oxford University Press, 1910.

*The Early Life of Mark Rutherford* (W. Hale White). By Himself. London: Humphrey Milford, Oxford University Press, 1913.

*Last Pages from a Journal With Other Papers.* By Mark Rutherford. Edited by His Wife. London: Humphrey Milford, Oxford University Press, 1915.

*Letters to Three Friends.* London: Humphrey Milford, Oxford University Press, 1924.

2. Translated and Edited Works

*Ethic Demonstrated in Geometrical Order and Divided into Five Parts, which treat I. Of God. II. Of the Nature and Origin of the Mind. III. Of the Origin and Nature of the Affects. IV. Of Human Bondage, or of the Strength of the Affects. V. Of the Power of the Intellect, or of Human Liberty. By Benedict De Spinoza.* Translated from the Latin By William Hale White. London: Trübner & Co., 1883.

*Tractatus de Intellectus Emendatione et de Via, Qua Optime in Veram Rerum Cognitionem Dirigitur.* Translated from the Latin of Benedict De Spinoza By W. Hale White. Translation revised by Amelia Hutchison Stirling, M.A. (Edin.). London: T. Fisher Unwin, 1895.

*The Inner Life of the House of Commons.* By William White. Edited with a Preface by Justin McCarthy, M.P., and with an Introduction by the Author's Son. 2 vols. London: T. Fisher Unwin, 1897.

*A Description of the Wordsworth & Coleridge Manuscripts in the Possession of Mr. T. Norton Longman.* Edited with Notes by W. Hale White. London: Longmans, Green & Co., 1897.

*Coleridge's Poems, A Facsimile Reproduction of the Proofs and MSS. of Some of the Poems.* Edited by the late James Dykes Campbell . . . With Preface and Notes by W. Hale White. Westminster: Archibald Constable and Co., 1899.

*Selections from Dr. Johnson's "Rambler."* Edited, with Preface and Notes by W. Hale White. Oxford: at the Clarendon Press, 1907.

*The Life of John Sterling.* By Thomas Carlyle, With an Introduction by W. Hale White. London: Henry Frowde, Oxford University Press, 1907.

3. The More Significant Unreprinted Contributions in Periodicals

"Births, Deaths, and Marriages," *Chamber's Journal*, IX (March 6, 1858), 155-57.

"The Priesthood *versus* the Human Mind and Science," *The Exeter and Plymouth Gazette*, January 6, 1864. Letter.

"House-Building," *The Spectator*, L (January 27, 1877), 113. Letter. Reprinted in Ruskin's *Fors Clavigera*.

## Selected Bibliography

"The Genius of Walt Whitman," *The Secular Review* (March 20, 1880).

"Marcus Antoninus," *The Secular Review* (July 3, 1880), pp. 5-6.

"Ixion," *The Secular Review* (September 11, 1880).

"Heathen Ethics," *The Secular Review* (November 27, 1880).

"What Mr. Emerson Owed to Bedfordshire," *The Athenaeum*, No. 2846 (May 13, 1882), 602-3.

"Letter on George Eliot," *The Athenaeum*, No. 3031 (November 28, 1885), 702.

"Our Debt to France," *The Bookman* (London), II (August, 1892), 139-40.

"Two Martyrs," *The Bookman* (London), III (February, 1893), 153-54.

"Dr. John Chapman," *The Athenaeum*, No. 3502 (December 8, 1894), 790-91.

"The Wilsonian Theory of Sunspots," *The Journal of the British Astronomical Association*, V (February 23, 1895), 218.

"Spinoza's Doctrine of the Relationship between Mind and Body," *The International Journal of Ethics*, VI (July 4, 1896), 515-18.

"Coleridge on Spinoza," *The Athenaeum*, No. 3630 (May 22, 1897), 680-81. Unpublished notes by Hale White.

Review of *The Poetical Works of William Wordsworth* (edited by William Knight, Vol. VIII, Macmillan & Co.), *The Athenaeum*, No. 3648 (September 25, 1897), 412-13.

"Misleading Unions," *The Pilot*, IV (July 20, 1901), 80-81. Letter.

"Tolstoï's Astronomy," *The Athenaeum*, No. 3870 (December 28, 1901), 879. Letter.

"Edward Fitzgerald on Carlyle's and Tennyson's Astronomy," *The Athenaeum*, No. 3881 (March 15, 1902), 388. Letter.

"Coleridge's Astronomy," *The Manchester Guardian*, May 3, 1902. Letter.

"Mr. W. S. Lilly and the *Times*," *The Speaker*, XIII (February 10, 1906), 457-58. Letter.

"The Golden Nail," *The Rochdale Observer*, February 17, 1906.

4. Regular Weekly Contributions in Newspapers

"Metropolitan Notes" (weekly column), the *Aberdeen Herald*, from May 11, 1861, to January 27, 1872.

"Below the Gangway" (weekly column), the *Morning Star* (London), from February 12, 1865, to July 10, 1866.

"Sketches in Parliament" (weekly column), the *Birmingham Journal*, the *Birmingham Daily Post and Journal* and the *Birmingham Daily Post* (these three changes in name occurred while Hale White wrote for this newspaper), from February 3, 1866, to January 31, 1880.

"Letters by a Radical" (weekly column), the *Rochdale Observer*, from January 19, 1867, to March 30, 1872.
"Sketches in Parliament" and "How it Strikes a Stranger" (weekly column), the *Nonconformist*, from February 14, 1872, to August 6, 1873.
"Our London Letter" (weekly column), the *Norfolk News*, from March 2, 1872, to March 17, 1883.

SECONDARY SOURCES

This is a selective listing of the more important available material on Hale White. For a fuller listing, see the Bibliography in Wilfred Stone, *Religion and Art of William Hale White*.

1. Critical and Biographical Works

BUCHMAN, URSULA CLARE. *William Hale White (Mark Rutherford). The Problem of Self-Adjustment in a World of Changing Values.* University of Zürich thesis. Zürich: Juris-Verlag, 1950. Touches on a variety of motifs in Hale White's writings.

KLINKE, HANS. *William Hale White, Versuch einer Biographie.* Griefswald dissertation. Frankfort: Wilhelm Bohn, 1930. A pioneering biographical work; still valuable.

MACLEAN, CATHERINE MACDONALD. *Mark Rutherford: A Biography of William Hale White.* London: Macdonald, 1955. The most detailed biography available in English.

STOCK, IRVIN. *William Hale White (Mark Rutherford). A Critical Study.* New York: Columbia University Press, 1956. Contains an introductory biographical sketch, discussions of the novels, and a selected bibliography.

STONE, WILFRED. *Religion and Art of William Hale White ("Mark Rutherford").* Stanford: Stanford University Press, 1954. A probing analysis of the work of Hale White in relation to his life and religion. A meticulous scholarly study, with the most complete bibliography available.

WHITE, DOROTHY V. *The Groombridge Diary.* London: Humphrey Milford, Oxford University Press, 1924. A detailed and intimate record of Hale White's last years: his thoughts, his conversation, his letters to Dorothy White. Essential for a complete understanding of him.

2. Essays in Books and Periodicals

BAKER, ERNEST A. "Mark Rutherford and Others." *The History of the English Novel.* London: H. F. and G. Witherby, Ltd., 1938,

## Selected Bibliography

IX, 97-121. Relates the absence of structure in the novels to the impression they convey of "authenticity" and "truth."

C. "The Art of Mark Rutherford." *The Academy*, LVI (February 4, 1899), 161-62. Discusses the style and the characterization in the novels.

CECIL, LADY ROBERT. "Mark Rutherford." *The Nation and Athenaeum*, XXXIV (October 27, 1923), 151-52. Contains the personal recollections of a friend: notes on Hale White's conversation, his reading, and his character.

DAWSON, WILLIAM JAMES. *The Makers of English Fiction*. New York: F. H. Revell Co., 1905. Discusses the novels as examples of "religious fiction."

HOWELLS, WILLIAM DEAN. "Editor's Study." *Harper's New Monthly Magazine*, LXXII (February, 1886), 485-86. A significant review, enthusiastic yet perceptive, of the first two novels.

LEVINE, GEORGE. "*The Cocktail Party* and *Clara Hopgood*." *The Graduate Student of English*, I (Winter, 1958), 4-11. Shows that Hale White's presentation of sainthood is more effective than T. S. Eliot's.

LOW, FRANCES H. "Mark Rutherford: An Appreciation." *The Fortnightly Review*, XC (September 1, 1908), 458-73. Stresses the "philosophical" quality of the novels and the "presentative power" of the characterizations.

MAISON, MARGARET. "Two Distinguished Doubters: Mark Rutherford and Robert Elsmere." *Search Your Soul Eustace. A Survey of the Religious Novel in the Victorian Age*. London: Sheed and Ward, 1961. Discusses the first two novels as spiritual confessions.

MASSINGHAM, H. W. "Memorial Introduction." *The Autobiography of Mark Rutherford*. London: T. Fisher Unwin, 1923. An excellent sketch of the character of the novels, noting their special place in Victorian fiction. One of the best essays.

MERTON, STEPHEN. "The Autobiographical Novels of Mark Rutherford." *Nineteenth-Century Fiction*, V (December, 1950), 189-207. This and the following three articles are incorporated in the present work.

———. "The Personality of Mark Rutherford." *Nineteenth-Century Fiction*, VI (June, 1951), 1-20.

———. "Mark Rutherford: The World of the Novels." *Bulletin of the New York Public Library*, LXVII (September, 1963), 470-78.

———. "George Eliot and William Hale White." *The Victorian Newsletter*, No. 25 (Spring, 1964), 13-15.

"Mid-Victorian Church and Chapel." *Living Age*, CCLXIII (November 6, 1909), 369-71. Compares Trollope's and Hale White's fictional presentation of the clergy and the religious attitudes of provincial England.

MURRY, JOHN MIDDLETON. "The Religion of Mark Rutherford." *The Adelphi*, II (July, 1924), 93-104. Sees Hale White's religion to be expressed in the very texture of his work.

NICOLL, W. ROBERTSON. "Memories of Mark Rutherford." *A Bookman's Letters*. London: Hodder and Stoughton, 1915. Contains the author's personal recollections of Hale White and summaries of the periodical writing on political and literary subjects.

SECCOMBE, THOMAS. "The Literary Works of Mark Rutherford." *Living Age*, CCLXXVII (May 24, 1913), 498-501. Deals with the religious-political aspects of the novels.

SPERRY, WILLARD L. "Mark Rutherford." *The Harvard Theological Review*, VII (April, 1914), 166-73. A comprehensive and incisive analysis of the novels. One of the best essays.

STOCK, IRVIN. "André Gide, William Hale White and the Protestant Tradition." *Accent*, XII (Autumn, 1952), 205-15. Sees an affinity between the two in their moral emphases and in their treatment of self-indulgence *vs.* self-sacrifice.

STONE, WILFRED H. "Browning and 'Mark Rutherford.'" *The Review of English Studies*, IV (n.s.) (July, 1953), 249-59. Discusses the personal acquaintance of the two men.

―――. "The Confessional Fiction of Mark Rutherford." *University of Toronto Quarterly*, XXIII (October, 1953), 35-57. Discusses the sources and development of themes in the novels.

TAYLOR, A. E. "The Novels of Mark Rutherford." *Essays and Studies by Members of the English Association*, V (1914), 51-74. Delineates perceptively the theme and the style of the novels. One of the best essays.

TAYLOR, W. D. "Mark Rutherford." *Queen's Quarterly*, XXV (October, 1917), 153-71. A discriminating account of the novels, with emphasis on the themes of political reform and human suffering.

TEMPEST, E. V. "Optimism in 'Mark Rutherford.'" *The Westminster Review*, CLXXX (August, 1913), 174-84. Shows the ways toward reconciliation presented in Hale White's work. A thoughtful essay.

WILLEY, BASIL. *The Eighteenth Century Background. Studies on the Idea of Nature in the Thought of the Period*. London: Chatto and Windus, 1946. Discusses Hale White's work as it throws light on Wordsworth's concept of nature.

―――. "'Mark Rutherford' (William Hale White)." *More Nineteenth Century Studies*. New York: Columbia University Press, 1956. A comprehensive, compact account of Hale White and his novels.

# *Index*

Aquinas, St. Thomas, 141
Arnold, Matthew, 21, 23, 33, 37, 40, 54, 64, 72, 137, 142, 147, 151, 153, 158, 159-60, 163
Austen, Jane, 35

Bach, Johann Sebastian, 27
Bacon, Francis, 32
Baxter, Richard, 60
Beckett, Samuel, 65
Beethoven, Ludwig van, 27, 59, 120
Bennett, Arnold, 133, 163
Bentham, Jeremy, 57
Bible, 26, 50, 51, 52, 157, 163
Blake, William, 68
Booth, William, 67, 145
Broad Church Movement, 87, 142
Brontë, Charlotte, 158-59, 160
Bunyan, John, 21, 35, 60, 63, 73, 81, 103, 150, 151, 157, 162
Burne-Jones, Edward, 27
Burns, Robert, 81, 157
Butler, Samuel, 34, 142
Byron, George Gordon, 23, 39, 40, 75, 80, 81, 82, 157, 158, 159, 160

Calvin, John, 30
Calvinism, 22, 37, 42, 54, 90, 137, 141
Carlyle, Thomas, 28, 30, 31, 32, 33, 39, 40, 44, 50, 53, 65, 72, 75, 78, 79, 88, 142, 145, 149, 157, 159, 160
Cazamian, Louis, 25
Cecil, Lady Robert, 61
Chapman, John, 25, 57-58
Chartism, 75, 79, 149
Chaucer, Geoffrey, 157
Chesterfield, Philip, Earl of, 164
Chopin, Frédéric, 27
Christian Socialism, 67, 142, 145
Clough, Arthur Hugh, 37

Cobbett, William, 46, 60
Coleridge, Samuel Taylor, 142
Constable, John, 34
Cromwell, Oliver, 21, 35
Cross, J. W., 31

Dante Alighieri, 109
Defoe, Daniel, 60
*De Imitationi Christi* (Kempis), 70, 150
Dewey, John, 162
Dickens, Charles, 33, 34, 72, 77, 138, 149
Dickinson, Emily, 21
Donne, John, 157
Dryden, John, 157

Eliot, George, 25, 27, 30, 31, 34, 35, 38, 39, 40, 58-59, 70, 82, 89, 91, 145, 151
Emerson, Ralph Waldo, 159
Epictetus, 64

Feuerbach, Ludwig, 145
French Revolution, 78, 80

Gide, Andre, 44, 163
Gissing, George, 23, 68, 163
Glanvill, Joseph, 164
Glück, Christoph Willibald von, 59
Goethe, Johann Wolfgang von, 23, 120, 150
Gosse, Edmund, 48, 163
Gray, Thomas, 35

Hardy, Thomas, 23, 138
Hazlitt, William, 158
Hegel, Wilhelm Friedrich, 141
Hemingway, Ernest, 163
Hilliard, Reverend Samuel, 39
Homer, 159
Hopkins, Gerard Manley, 21

Howells, William Dean, 33, 139, 163
Hughes, Arthur, 27
Hunt, Holman, 27

Ibsen, Henrik, 38, 121, 124

James, Henry, 137
James, William, 90, 143
Johnson, Samuel, 157
Jukes, Reverend John, 39, 85

Keats, John, 33, 150
Kilvert, Francis, 21, 164
Kingsley, Charles, 45, 67, 68, 142, 145

*Leben Jesu* (Strauss), 57, 120
Lewis, Sinclair, 121
*Lyrical Ballads* (Wordsworth and Coleridge), 22, 49, 50, 95, 144

Maclean, Catherine Macdonald, 62
Marcus Aurelius, 64
Massingham, H. W., 28
Maurice, F. D., 45, 67, 68, 142, 145
Mazzini, Giuseppe, 132-33, 148
Mill, John Stuart, 49, 57, 121, 123, 147
Millais, John Everett, 27
Milton, John, 28, 29, 40, 115, 121, 123, 157
Mitford, Nancy, 35
Moore, George, 163
More, Henry, 164
Morris, Caleb, 39-40, 55
Morris, William, 27
Mozart, Wolfgang Amadeus, 27

Naturalism, 163
Newman, John Henry, 40, 54
Nicoll, William Robertson, 27, 124

Oxford Movement, 142

Paine, Thomas, 81
Pascal, Blaise, 144
Pater, Walter, 109
Plato, 152

Pope, Alexander, 157
Pre-Raphaelites, 27, 29, 33

Randall, John Herman, Jr., 143, 162
Ritschl, Albrecht, 142
Rossetti, D. G., 27
Rousseau, Jean Jacques, 81
Ruskin, John, 27, 28, 40, 47, 67, 72, 105, 145, 149, 159

St. Paul, 48, 50, 82, 95, 109, 115, 118
Santayana, George, 145
Schleiermacher, Friedrich, 142, 145
Scott, Walter, 81, 93, 158
Seccombe, Thomas, 39
Shaftesbury, Anthony, Earl of, 164
Shakespeare, William, 23, 30, 63, 111, 157
Shaw, Bernard, 124
Shelley, Percy Bysshe, 77, 78, 157, 160
Socialism, 147
Spenser, Edmund, 23, 157
Sperry, William Learoyd, 35, 61
Spinoza, Benedict de, 30, 64, 65, 126, 127, 150-53, 154

Tennyson, Alfred, 37, 122, 123, 156
Thackeray, William Makepeace, 34
Thompson, James, 23
Thoreau, Henry David, 21
Tillich, Paul, 162
Tolstoy, Leo, 157
Trilling, Lionel, 137, 151
Trollope, Anthony, 34, 35

*Ulysses* (Joyce), 126

Wagner, Wilhelm Richard, 27
Walker, Fred, 27
Wesley, John, 54
*Westminster Review*, 57
White, Mrs. Dorothy Vernon (second wife of Hale White), 22, 24, 25, 26, 27, 31, 32, 36, 42, 156
White, William (father of Hale White), 27, 40, 45-46, 52, 60, 61, 66, 68, 79

## Index

White William Hale, his working day, 21-22, 69; seriousness, 22-23; melancholy, 23-24; reticence, 24-26, 42-43; interest in painting and music, 26-28; "Puritanism," 28-30; iconoclasm, 30-33; the world of his novels, 33-41; his religion, 37, 49-52, 90, 95, 110, 114, 119, 120, 128, 140-45, 161-62; his heroes 39, 76, 89; his work in the Admiralty, 43, 62-63, 71-72; relations with his father, 44-46, 48; his childhood, 46-48, 71; his "conversion," 48; college career, 49-52; his style, 60-61, 138, 139, 162-63; his journalistic writing, 66; interest in astronomy, 90, 98-99, 153-57; political thought, 145-49; philosophical thought, 149-53. literary criticism, 157-60

WRITINGS OF:

*Argument for an Extension of the Franchise, An*, 75, 148-49
*Autobiography of Mark Rutherford, The*, 22, 23, 33, 35, 36, 37, 42-61, 63, 65, 69, 70, 73, 74, 76, 86, 94, 96, 102, 107, 117, 120, 125, 141, 142, 144, 154, 158
"Byron, Goethe, and Mr. Matthew Arnold," 75
*Catharine Furze*, 28, 33, 36, 103-19, 128, 129
*Clara Hopgood*, 32, 59, 120-34, 143, 152
"Confessions of a Self Tormentor," 25
"Dream of Two Dimensions, A," 135

*Early Life of Mark Rutherford*, 34, 44, 45, 51, 52, 57, 68, 100, 141
*Ethic* of Spinoza translated and discussed, 63, 127, 149, 150, 152, 153
*John Bunyan*, 30
"Marcus Antoninus," 64
*Mark Rutherford's Deliverance*, 38, 43, 44, 56, 59, 62-74, 75, 87, 93, 96, 102, 126, 142, 146, 150
"Michael Trevanion," 135-36
*Miriam's Schooling*, 25, 32, 56, 89-102, 112, 130, 143, 154-55
"Morality of Byron's Poetry, The," 76, 158
"Mr. Whitaker's Retirement," 139
"Mysterious Portrait, A," 136-37, 138
"Notes on the Book of Job," 64
"Notes on Shelley's Birthplace," 77
"Our Debt to France," 78
"Preacher and the Sea, The," 161
"Principles," 65
"Revolution," 153
*Revolution in Tanner's Lane, The*, 22, 38, 55, 67, 74, 75-88, 89, 102, 112, 141, 146, 147, 154
"Wilsonian Theory of Sunspots, The," 156
Wollstonecraft, Mary, 121
Wordsworth, Dorothy, 27, 59, 164
Wordsworth, William, 23, 26, 30, 33, 36, 40, 49, 50, 55, 65, 73, 78, 94, 111, 123, 135, 137, 146, 151, 153, 154, 157, 160
Wright, Frank Lloyd, 163

Zola, Emile, 163